GREEK
FOLK
SONGS

Greek
Folk
Songs

Translated by
Joshua Barley

With a Foreword by
A. E. Stallings

AIORA

[Handwritten inscription:]

31st August 2022

For Sally,

Looking forward to hearing you sing some of these! with love from

Josh

We would like to thank Mr Pantelis Boukalas for editing the Greek texts and for his comments on the selection of songs. Thanks are also due to Professor David Ricks for his detailed comments on the introduction and translations.

Joshua Barley is a translator of modern Greek literature and writer. He read Classics at Oxford and modern Greek at King's College, London. His translations of Ilias Venezis' *Serenity* and Makis Tsitas' *God Is My Witness* are published by Aiora Press. *A Greek Ballad*, selected poems of Michális Ganás (translated with David Connolly), is published by Yale University Press.

Illustrations by Panagiotis Stavropoulos

ISBN: 978-618-5369-62-0

First edition by Aiora Press, July 2022.

AIORA PRESS
11 Mavromichali St.
Athens 10679 - Greece
tel: +30 210 3839000
www.aiorabooks.com

CONTENTS

FOREWORD

The anonymous Greek folk songs—the "demotic songs"—are not only a deep spring from which modern Greek literature draws, they form a bedrock of the modern Greek vernacular itself and the centuries-old roots of a young national identity.

All the more surprising then, that for all their import, lyric vigor, and scholarly interest, this volume marks the first significant collection of the songs to appear in English in over a century.

Only two previous major English verse translations of the songs exist at all,[1] the earliest translated not from the Greek, but from the French of Claude Charles Fauriel's seminal *Chants Populaires de la Grèce moderne.* Fauriel's project, which appeared in 1824, the year of Byron's death in Messolonghi, was published to stir up Western sympathy for the Greek War of Independence against the Ottoman Turks (1821–29). The London Greek Committee immediately commissioned an English translation in support of the Greek cause. Appearing

---

[1] Where Greek folk songs have appeared in translation in recent years, the focus has been on the living tradition of the songs, along with their music and dances, such as Gail Holst-Warhaft's *Nisiotika* (2021), or on personal reminiscences of the tradition, such as Thomas Scotes' *Weft of Memory: A Greek Mother's Recollections of Folksongs, Poems and Proverbs* (2008), in which the author collects Greek folk songs and oral history as told and sung by his mother, Vasiliki Scotes.

in 1825, Charles Brinsley Sheridan's *The Songs of Greece* consisted of versions nativized into robust ballads in a style familiar to English audiences from the popular 1798 *Lyrical Ballads* of Wordsworth and Coleridge and the 1803 *Minstrelsy of the Scottish Border* of Sir Walter Scott. At a double remove from the Greek, Sheridan's versions are rousing as verse, but bear little resemblance to the 'originals' (if such a word is appropriate for a largely oral tradition).

After Sheridan's volume, no new English collection of the songs would appear until over seventy years later, in 1896, the year of the first modern Olympics, inaugurated in Athens. The second, and, up to now, the last verse translation of the songs, was the work of English folklorist, anthropologist, and intrepid traveler Lucy Garnett, better known for her study, *Turkey of the Ottomans*. Her *Greek Folk Poesy* is impressive in scholarship and ambitious in scope. Weighing in at four hundred pages, and largely the result of Garnett's own research, it contains little to no overlap with Fauriel's collection.

Garnett, proficient in modern Greek, translated the lyrics not only with accuracy, but into the selfsame fifteen-syllable iambic meter. But her use of the archaisms, inversions, and conventions of (again) Scott's border ballads led to stilted and infelicitous results. The slippage between fleet-footed, polysyllabic Greek and marching English monosyllables invited repetition and filler. Consider her opening of "The Fruit of the Apple Tree":

> With all his greyhounds fleet around, a youth goes out a-hunting
> A falcon small upon his wrist he bears as forth he sallies.
> It frees itself and flies afar and in a garden enters;
> But quick, his falcon to regain, the hunter follows after.
> A maiden fair he finds within, at marble basin washing;
> With whitest pearls she is bedecked, and many golden sequins.
> 'Call off thy dogs, sir Hunter bold, and tie them to the bushes!

None of this is wrong, but it is misleading; the Greek, natural in syntax, is also straightforward, almost *modern*, in language. The "maiden fair" is simply a "girl," she addresses the hunter only as "hunter" (not "sir Hunter bold"), and she asks him to gather his dogs and tie them to a "little tree." Even the falling meter, natural in Greek, feels here strained and affected, and is presumably what is driving the questionable choice of "bushes."

W.B. Yeats, who reviewed the book, was not impressed. While interested in the book's preface by John Stuart-Glennie (expounding on a dubious theory of race and civilization), when it comes to the translations themselves, Yeats laments, "A scientific theory can but suffer a temporary injury from the language of its exposition, but a folk song put into bad verse loses the half of its scientific and nearly all its literary interest." Ms. Garnett could have made a better book, he suggests, by sticking to prose. (Perhaps inspired by this very review, an outlier prose version of Greek folk songs does appear four years later, in 1900.)

In the end, though, Yeats decides it is at least partly the fault of the Greek songs themselves, too "civilized" for their own good, and without the elemental energy of more "primitive" Romanian or Gaelic folk songs. Certainly Garnett has tamed or domesticated her sources, as we see in the example above. But something of their charm seems to have rubbed off on Yeats in spite of himself. He later admits that "The Song of Wandering Aengus" ("The silver apples of the moon / The golden apples of the sun") is inspired by a Greek folk song, perhaps even this very one, which ends with the maiden's white pearls and gold sequins compared to a windfall of apples.

Yeats views the folk songs through his own fascination with Gaelic folk songs and traditions. People with an interest in Classical Greece likewise tend to look at them through perceived connections with ancient poems and myth. In this, I am no different. It is irresistible to ponder, even if impossible to solve, whether such connections are folk memory, convergent cultural evolution, platonic archetypes, shared imagination, coincidence, or some serendipitous amalgam thereof. Death as Charos/Charon and a Hades/underworld that doesn't map onto Christian theology is just one example.

In "The Return of the Long-Lost Husband," for instance, the conversation between the long-wandering husband and his waiting wife as she seeks to establish his identity so closely resembles the scene between Penelope and Odysseus in book twenty-three of the *Odyssey* that it seems impossible there should be no connection, perhaps especially when we consider the lexical as well as situational parallels. In the song, the Greek word for a mole or birthmark—the marks/signs (σημάδια) on the "trunk" of the wife's body (κορμιού), which should be unknown to any man but her husband—is "olive," "ελιά." Odysseus in Homer also offers a secret identifying sign (σῆμα) too, something only they as a couple could know, that their marriage bed is made from a rooted olive tree (ἐλαίns); he had hewn the bed from its living trunk (κορμὸν) himself. If the connection between these two passages is uncanny and mysterious (one could almost see the reading of olive tree in the *Odyssey* as a brilliant metaphorical misreading for "birthmark," a sign that would more aptly parallel Odysseus's scar), the multiple points of contact point to more than a hunch.

Or consider the song of exile, "The Witch," where the far-off husband cannot return to his wife because a witch has him in her clutches:

> Marry if you want to—or become a nun,
> but in these wretched places, I'm a married man.
> The woman that I've taken is a crafty witch,
> who bewitches all the boats so they do not set out,
> and she's bewitched me also, and nor do I set out.

It is hard not to think of Circe here, winding Odysseus around her enchanted finger and holding him for years on her island. Circe is of course an immortal goddess—perhaps she is still out there up to her old tricks on Pelion (the setting of the modern song). Or maybe traveling men continue to make the same excuses they always have.

In these songs, Death arrives on horseback. The association between horses and death goes back at least to the geometric era (c. 900–700 BCE); horses are sacrificed at graves, and horses are a common depiction on funerary pots. But the metaphor, even kenning, whereby a coffin is a wooden horse inevitably reminds us that in Greek, the Trojan horse is never referred to as such, but as the "wooden" horse. Again, there is something uncanny in how the more modern metaphor seems to anachronistically flash insight into an ancient myth. Is not the Trojan horse a kind of coffin, a nightmare pregnant with death in its flanks?

But in the personification of death itself, the anonymous songs not only connect to the afterlife of the Classical pagan past, they cover new ground, inventing a kind of fairy-tale mythology of their own. Death (Charos/Charon) is not merely arrived at, by the living, who come to his invisible realm ("Hades" may connect, etymologically, with "un-seen"), he seeks them out on his black horse, or sometimes carries them off on a ship. He can be argued with but tends to have the last word. In "The Keys to the Underworld," reminiscent of the story of Bluebeard, complete with keys and severed heads, Charos grants the speaker's wish to look into the underworld, only to see

the young men weaponless, the girls without their braids;
. . . the darling little children rotting like withered apples,
. . . the good housewives like doors torn off their hinges.

The withered apples! The women like torn-away doors! One image reeks of a spoiled sweetness, the other devastates with its violence, domestic and brutal. The doors torn away remind me of famous icons of the Harrowing of Hell, where Jesus pulls Adam and Eve from their graves, and the gates of hell lie broken underfoot, beneath the earth with a scattering of keys and hardware. But in the song there is no suggestion of a Christian resurrection, only ruin and unmaking.

These bold new settings, in a direct, un-fusty English vernacular, with a weather eye on the "originals" and a poet's ear for the line, are not only welcome, but overdue. Barley approaches the songs as lyric and literature; here they are stripped of political agenda and are free from the academic concerns of early folklorists. He possesses a contagious joy in their rich language, efficient narrative, and inventive metaphors, in their human rather than national dimension, even as he places them within the context of the rituals and traditions of village life. With the generous inclusion of the Greek, this treasury should mark a new era of interest in, and influence by, these songs for twenty-first-century Anglophone poets, song writers, and translators, even as they have inspired poets, Greek and non-Greek alike, in the past.

A. E. Stallings

INTRODUCTION:

Questions of an Oral Tradition

Who?

The first life of the folk songs took place in villages throughout the Greek world, over the course of many centuries. Some came of age in the Byzantine Empire (330–1453 CE); others in the centuries of Ottoman rule that followed. The villages that mothered them extended far beyond what is now Greece: from parts of southern Italy (Calabria) to Eastern Turkey (notably the Black Sea coast—the Pontus—and Cappadocia), Cyprus, Crete, the islands of the Aegean and Ionian seas and the mountains of the Greek and Balkan mainland. These settlements were often isolated and remote, but in necessary communication with each other via extensive networks of cobbled mule tracks or plied routes in the trackless sea, and through the common conduit of the Greek language.

The 'folk' of these villages followed a traditional way of life, based on agriculture, seafaring and trade, which remained largely unchanged regardless of whether there was a Christian emperor or a Muslim sultan in Constantinople or Istanbul (in the idealized world of the folk songs, the ultimate authority is always the *vasilias*, the king). Allegiance was first to the family, and then to the village. It is the challenges and ruptures in these cocoon-units (whether through death, marriage or leaving to work abroad) that inspire much of the material of the songs.

The limited literacy entailed an oral culture, in which the principal modes of understanding the world, or of escaping it, were storytelling or singing. Singing accompanied every activity, from working in the fields to travel between villages, to the formal rituals that sanctified marriage and death. In this world, there was a song to enact, legitimize, encase or simply embroider every activity, any time of the day, any time of the year.

As works of oral composition, the songs must be understood in a radically different way from written literature. Since the work of Milman Parry and Albert Lord on Homeric epic, most scholarship tells us that oral poetry has no single author, no single 'original', nor does it express an individual's point of view. Likewise, these modern Greek folk songs are mainly products of the community as a whole, composed collectively, expressing the communal view, and passed down with slow (if any) development through the generations. It might be helpful to think of the system of folk songs as a language, rather than as individual creations. Language is not created by individuals, nor can its roots be traced to individuals. And each user of a language, like the singer of the songs, must stick to a particular grammar, which has been worked out over centuries and which carries within it an embedded collective philosophy and social function.

A mother's lament for her dead child, therefore, can be sung by a woman who has no blood connection to the family. Her lament, even if sung in the first person, is not expressing private grief: rather, it is a formulated strategy, with the words sanctioned by ritual as much as the other funeral rites. Take these lines, from one of the laments:

But you, dear eyes, deserve nine women to lament you,
three of them from Yannena, three of them from Arta
and three of them from your own land, three who know your name.

Certain women, then, achieved the status of professional lamenters. There were professional singers and musicians, too, who performed at the village festivals (*paniyiria*) throughout the Greek world and played a large role in dispersing the songs. But unlike other oral cultures, and unlike in ancient Greece, such bards did not play the primary role in the composition of songs (with the exception of the so-called *poiitarides* of Cyprus). The women working at their looms were as likely to be the crafters and vehicles of songs as professional singers.

What?

The songs form a protean corpus. Even to class them all as songs is a later construct by literate folklorists. The singers would hardly have spoken of a ritual lament in the same terms as a dance song at a festival. Nonetheless, they are bound together by the world from which they derive and by the inhabitants of that world who used them. For the stranger, therefore, it is inevitable—and essential—that a map be drawn.

N.G. Politis (1852–1921), the founder of the discipline of *laografia* (the study of folklore) in Greece, established fourteen categories of folk song. They include historical songs (*istorika*), brigand songs (*kleftika*), ballads (*paraloges*), love songs (*tis agapis*), marriage songs (*nyfiatika*), lullabies (*nanarismata*), songs of Greeks far from home (*tis xeniteias*), laments (*miroloyia*) and laments of the underworld and Charos (*miroloyia tou kato kosmou kai tou Charou*). Some of these labels have subsequently been considered problematic, but they have formed the basis of almost all collections and anthologies since Politis put them forward in 1909. Politis' own anthology of the songs—*Selections from the Songs of the Greek people* (1914)—remains in print and highly popular.

In this book I have made use of many of Politis' categories, sometimes eliding two or more into each of the five sections. All aspects of life were examined and processed by the collective mind of the singers; I have unavoidably left many holes in that broad tapestry. Such omissions include songs that accompanied work (*ergatika*), prison songs (*tis fylakis*) and songs that marked religious festivals (*kalanda*), as well as obscene and satirical songs, which most early collectors shied away from. My intention has been to find the songs with the richest, most imaginative and varied poetry, rather than provide a cross section of old village life.

The songs printed here are drawn from various collections and anthologies compiled over the last two hundred years, from the first published collection of Greek folk songs by Claude Charles Fauriel in 1824, to Politis' aforementioned anthology of 1914, to modern anthologies that have taken their material from the evergrowing archive of the Hellenic Folklore Research Centre in Athens.

Almost all of these anthologies focus exclusively on the words of the songs, rather than their musical or performative aspects. As such, various features of the original songs are lost—even apart from the obvious differences between performed songs and written texts. For example, some of the songs would have included short refrains (*yirismata*—'turnings') when sung, or single words repeated in the middle of lines (*tsakismata*—'cuttings'). Only one song in this book ('For Dimos') retains these marks of oral performance.

Another crucial feature of oral composition is the concept of variation: the song can be sung differently with every performance, generating an endless array of variants (called *parallages* in Greek). Even the same singer, when asked to perform the same song twice, might sing it differently. By contrast, the text on the page gives the false appearance of fixed, final stability. Some scholars have suggested ways of incorporating the idea of variation into the written texts (for example, setting out songs as a table, with alternative progressions). I have not done so. Rather I have selected, as far as possible, the variant that I felt expressed the themes of the song most skilfully and completely.

Equally absent from a written collection is the social function and context of the song. Functional differences between songs would have been the primary means of classification for the original singers: a song could be danced to (*choreftiko*), usually at the annual village festival, or recited while seated, 'at the table' (*tis tavlas*), or performed as part of a specific ritual, such as a funeral.

Reading a lament outside the setting of a death alters its intended effect and affect. The words themselves may refer to the stages of the ritual, meaning that they cannot be fully understood without some knowledge of it. In the case of laments, the different stages of the funeral are often invoked, from the laying out of the body in the deceased's house, surrounded by flowers and fruit, to the wake, to the final journey to the grave and, finally, the burial. The words come to life when imagined in their original setting, such as in one of the encomiums:

...lay her down on the grass, in May's own lovely garden,
so that the blossom falls over her, apples in her apron,
and let the red carnations lie strewn around her hair.

Much is lost, therefore, in written versions of songs: from the smell of apples to the note of the clarinet to the sweat of the dancer beside you. And yet the songs thrive too as written poems—a fact that has been recognized ever since they were first collected, and was praised, for example, by Goethe. This book accepts that they can now be considered as texts, in the same way that the songs of Sappho are texts. Severed from their original function, they are as enriching to the reader as they were life-constituting to their first singers and listeners.

When?

There is an essential difficulty in dating songs of an oral tradition, since they have no fixed form and are constantly subject to change. New elements can and do accrue to old themes over time. Similar difficulties might be encountered in attempting to date words or phrases of a language. What makes the terrain even more treacherous is the fact that the chronology of the songs has always been a politicized question, since it entails the issue of cultural continuity with ancient Greece: the prime motivation for the first collecting of folk songs was to find a cultural link between the ancient Greeks and the people of the modern nation. Philhellenes, scholars and nationalists have therefore sought —and found, with varying claims to authenticity—relics of classical Greek culture in these songs. Setting aside these politicized issues, there are ways to unravel the layered history of these songs.

Among the most ancient of the songs are the ritual laments. Indeed, it was the laments that the first Greek scholars had recourse to when arguing for continuation from ancient Greece: Spyridon Zambelios (1813–81) argued for a continuation from ancient tragedy to modern Greek 'song' (*tragoudi*) via the laments. And a classic study by Margaret Alexiou[2] has traced the continuation of funeral rites, and the words that accompany them, from antiquity to modern times. In the intervening centuries, customs and beliefs lived side by side with the Orthodox Christian tradition. Reading the laments, it is clear that the perception of death and the afterlife (in the underworld) is untouched by a Christian Heaven. From one of the songs of the underworld:

---

[2] Margaret Alexiou, *The Ritual Lament in Greek Tradition*, Cambridge University Press, 1974.

and if you ask I'll tell you about the underworld,
where the white is turned to black, where the rosy-cheeked pale,
and where the lovely-faced lose their lovely looks.

Even if the details have been developed in laments such as this one, the fundamental idea of Hades as a vast, empty, ill-lit, unwatered space, with wretched shades wandering in perpetuity, has persisted. This bleak vision dates to pre-Christian times.

Other indicators of chronology can be mined from the imagery of the laments. The personification of death, Charos—whose ancestry ultimately goes back to Charon, the ancient ferryboatman of the River Styx in the underworld—appears in some of the most striking songs of the canon as a violent criminal, a plundering corsair or invader. The imagery is drawn from the widespread piracy and multitude of foreign invasions that marked the later years of the Byzantine Empire and early years of Ottoman rule (fifteenth to eighteenth century). The French scholar Guy Saunier has taken this conclusion further and suggested that a sense of injustice (*adikia*), linked to the feeling of oppression in the Greek villages during this era, marks the poetics of much of the corpus. Over the centuries, he argues, the mythology of the underworld and Charos became progressively more violent, despairing and inhumane. From one of the songs of Charos:

Charos from a lofty peak came roaming down the mountain,
and set up his pavilion in the upper neighbourhood.

It is entirely possible, then, that a theme dating back to ancient Greece will be stitched together with one from medieval times (say, Charos as a knight) or from Ottoman times (Charos as an invader).

The other set of songs that are commonly held to have ancient roots are the ballads, which often seem to contain traces of ancient, even

archetypal myth. One theory, put forward in the middle of the twentieth century, is that ancient Greek myths and stories survived into
Roman times in the form of popular, pantomime-like theatre. The ballads, it is argued, represent the modern continuation of this tradition.

Among these shifting sands, the 'brigand songs' (*kleftika*) provide
a patch of more solid ground: even though they no doubt have a much
longer history, the songs preserved today are tied to a particular historical moment, which is the struggle for dominance over mountainous areas of the Greek mainland in the late seventeenth to early
nineteenth centuries. They are often more easily dateable, given the
presence of known historical brigands; some of them, too, are by the
hand of individuals. Many of the songs of Greeks far from home date
from the same period, when the exodus of Greeks from the mainland
to the Balkans reached its apogee. Such historical and sociological
factors help to make chronological divisions among what is ultimately
a medley of popular belief, social custom and storytelling, honed over
millennia.

The oral tradition that bore these songs is only precariously alive in
Greece. Like a language, though even more fragile, oral tradition dies
when its speakers stop using it. In the case of Greek folk song, the
speakers of that language were illiterate villagers in exceptionally close-
knit communities. Such communities do not exist in Greece anymore.
The sea changes in Greek village society, through the 1960s and 1970s
—including the advent of literacy, mechanized transport, radio and
television—spelt the end of the way of life that enabled collective composition. Remnants of the tradition are to be found on the islands of
Crete and Carpathos, where productive traditions of improvising
rhyming couplets (*mantinades*) still flourish. Despite the brilliance and
wit of these couplets, free improvisation and rhyme are the hallmarks
of an oral tradition in decline, since they imply that the established
themes of the old tradition are no longer productive.

The demise of oral composition does not mean that folk songs cannot be heard in Greece. There are parts of Greece where young people are learning traditional instruments and songs with more gusto than ever. They compose their own songs, too. But they cannot be classed in the same tradition as the songs of this book, since they are not products of oral composition. Still, many of the songs contained here (with the exception of the laments) can be heard in some form at festivals throughout the country, mixed with more modern creations. They are still danced to beneath the plane tree in the village square. But they are bottled, not running water. The society that created them has gone, and the ability to create new works—or rather, develop the existing ones—has gone with it.

Where?

The geographical origins of the songs are often as untraceable as their chronology. Despite the fact that anthologies often assert locality (Cretan songs, say, or Epirot songs), many of the songs can be found in other regions as well, sometimes the whole of the Greek world. As a general rule, the older a song is, the wider its dispersal.

Local variation exists, naturally. There are particular ways of singing the same song that are associated with different places. The image of a man languishing on a mountainside in one of the songs of Greeks far from home, say, will readily become a man languishing on a seashore when the same song is sung on an island. More significant local styles emerged, too, such as the laments from the Mani region of the southern Peloponnese. These long and inventive works form a tradition all of their own, sung in a different metre from the other laments and involving more improvisation. The island of Cyprus also developed its own local traditions—regrettably there was not space to represent them in this book.

There are other sociological factors that influence the prevalence of certain songs in certain regions. The brigand songs given here, for example, are connected to the mountainous regions of mainland Greece: Epirus, Western Macedonia, Thessaly, Central Greece (particularly the mountainous Agrafa region) and, to a lesser extent, the Peloponnese. The brigands themselves lived and acted there, hence the songs were born and flourished there. Many of the songs of Greeks far from home share this mainland bias, as the conditions (particularly in Epirus) in the historical period described above, were liable to drive huge swathes of the population abroad.

Most of the ballads are found throughout the Greek world, thus providing another reason for us to consider them among the oldest songs in the canon. But to complicate matters, many of their stories are also found in other languages throughout the Balkans. A classic case is 'The Bridge of Arta', the tale of a master craftsman who must build his own wife into the foundations of the bridge to stop it falling down. The same story of sacrifice is found in Albanian, Serbian, Macedonian, Bulgarian, Romanian, Hungarian, Judeo-Spanish and even Aramaic folklore. Such wide distribution calls into question any nationalistic appropriation of the ballads, and suggests an even more ancient universal pool from which the stories were drawn.

The songs are sung in their local dialects, and it is a mark of authenticity to find the dialect rendered correctly in the anthologies. As such, some of the songs here are in a form of Greek that would be opaque to a contemporary Athenian. But one of the joys of these songs is to peel back the local dialects and find the same songs being sung in places as far removed as, say, Crete and eastern Turkey.

How?

Regardless of function, chronology and content, the fundamental building blocks of the songs remain the same. Most characteristic of all is the metre, which (with few exceptions) is the fifteen-syllable line, the iambic *dekapentasyllavos*, also called the *politikos stichos*. With its roots in Roman times, this metre has developed over the centuries to become inseparable from the folk songs. In turn, the metre has repaid this trust, shaping the style and the very language of the songs.

The fifteen syllables make up a line of two uneven halves, split by a strong *caesura* (break). The first half is made of four iambic or two-syllable 'feet', and the second is the same but with the final syllable missing, making the line end in a trochee. In other words, *da-dum da-dum da-dum da-dum / da-dum da-dum da-dum-dum*. These two asymmetrical halves serve as an effective means of balancing or contrasting two ideas.

> For every bell there was a priest, / for every priest a deacon.
> The sick were sitting in the stern, / the wounded in the prow
> A thousand men went out in front, / a thousand more behind him,

There is no enjambment (running over) between lines. Nor, in most cases, is there rhyme. Each line, or even half line, carries autonomous units of meaning. The independence of these fragments makes for the characteristically choppy discourse, and is crucial to the composition of oral poetry. As in Homer (and other oral traditions), these folk songs have certain 'stock' material, which can be shared between songs and help the singer remember a song or connect elements in it. The most obvious examples of the stock material are lines or half lines, repeated more or less word for word between songs, often called 'formulas':

'Three little partridges were perched'
'Then from a window up above'
'On Easter Day, a fine Sunday, a day to be remembered'
'the fine-drawn lines of eyebrows'

More subtly, the singer may draw on abstract patterns in which only a word or two are repeated, but in which the underlying structure of the syntax is the same. Such patterns may run over more than one line. A good example is the use of questions and answers. Compare, from a well-known song of Charos ('Charos and the Souls'),

Is it the wind that batters them, is it the rain that beats them?
It's not the wind that batters them, it's not the rain that beats them,

with

Is it wild beasts tussling, is it buffaloes butchered?
It's not wild beasts tussling, it's not buffaloes butchered;

from a brigand song ('Song of Boukovalas').

There are structures lying beneath these lines of a kind that written poetry has no need for. It is the combination of the various patterns and formulas that makes for the differences between song variants, or *parallages*. The singer's skill lies in the ability to stitch together the different formulas in accordance with the structural patterns. Improvisation is limited to the underlying set of rules; the singer cannot simply improvise a line of fifteen-syllable verse: she must stick to the patterns enshrined within the poetics established over time, always keeping within the bounds of the song in question, each of which has its own internal cohesion. In practice, as with any traditional craft (as within a language), there is considerable scope for personal style and art beyond vocal accomplishment.

On a larger scale, the songs share themes and images between them. A wife bidding goodbye to her house, family and neighbourhood at her marriage will become the lament of a deceased person leaving their house, family and neighbourhood in death; likewise, the image of a horse being prepared for departure in one of the songs of Greeks far from home will be applied to a lament, for the deceased's final journey to the grave. These images are refashioned or embellished with great inventiveness.

Linguistically, the folk songs are as virtuosic as any written poetry, and the fifteen-syllable metre has evidently been a driving force in linguistic innovation. The second half of the fifteen-syllable line, for example, has proven to be a kind of incubator for some of the most inventive compound words in the Greek language, some of which occupy the entire half line. *Εγλυκοτραγουδούσε* (*eglykotragoudouse*), 'she was sweetly singing', must ultimately derive from a phrase, but in the songs it becomes one word of seven syllables, slotting into the second half of the line. In one of the laments, we find the extraordinary (and equally long) compound *ηλιοσκαμαγκισμένε* (*ilioskamangismene*), literally meaning 'whose hair has been whitened like wool in the sun'. Many more examples could be given. From the astonishing production of such words, it can easily be claimed that the folk songs not only employ some of the most inventive language of all Greek literature, but that they have played their part in forming the language itself.

Over the centuries, the songs are augmented for the sake of a more detailed description, or pared down for the sake of economy and drama. The result is a collection of endlessly honed and crafted words, lines and images, which form songs of a very particular style. The lexicon and the vocabulary of metaphor have been defined by natural selection: a girl is simply called a *λυγερή* (*ligeri*—literally 'slender') or a μαυρομάτα (*mavromata*—'dark-eyed'), and a horse is simply a μαύρος (*mavros*—'black'). These are the stylized conventions of an oral tradition—a girl is by nature lovely, as a young man is brave and proud. Elliptical language is matched by economy of description and narrative: few adjectives (certainly no subjective ones) and no explanation on the course of events. Direct speech, usually without third-person linking passages, and intense repetition heighten the drama.

Like building a traditional village house, therefore, these songs make use of few raw materials and adhere to conventional structures. But such limitations have only served to enhance the beauty of their poetry.

JB

NOTE ON TRANSLATION

These English settings do not use a fixed metre. I have nonetheless tried to maintain the feeling of the Greek fifteen-syllable metre, which splits the line into two uneven halves, with four stresses in the first half and three in the second – as in English ballad metre.

I have also aimed to maintain other features of the Greek text, such as the autonomous nature of each half-line, the strange-sounding compound words and the sense of logical argument. I have kept a line-by-line correspondence with the Greek.

It has not been my intention to make the poems sound like English folk songs, even though some use of English 'folk' idiom has been useful. Nonetheless, I have always tried to imagine that the English words could be sung.

Greek
Folk
Songs

SONGS OF HISTORY AND BRIGANDS

This section combines two similar styles of song that are often classi-
fied separately. The historical songs (*istorika* in Greek) are a slippery
entity, recording various significant moments of history, such as
the fall of a city or the death of a hero in war. Those songs that have
retained currency tend to record such momentous events as the fall of
Constantinople, or the songs associated with heroes of the Greek War
of Independence. The brigand songs (*kleftika*), which make up the
rest of the section, have a narrower focus and a particular terse style.
The brigands they celebrate —sometimes called in English by their
Greek term, klefts—were outlaws, who formed bands in the mountains
of mainland Greece and lived from petty thieving, extortion or whole-
sale plundering of villages. The best of them became 'captains'—men-
at-arms— and were employed by the Ottoman authorities to protect
villages against banditry. In turn they fought for superiority with other
representatives of the Ottomans, particularly the Albanian–Muslim
pass guards, who guarded strategic mountain passes. These conflicts,
which culminated in the wars waged by the Albanian-born tyrant Ali
Pasha (1740-1822) at the turn of the nineteenth century against
captains and brigands, were later seen as a precursor to the Greek
War of Independence. Many brigands, or former brigands, played a
central role in that war and hence became hailed as national heroes.

Άλωσις της Κωνσταντινουπόλεως

Πήραν την Πόλιν, πήρανε, πήραν το Σαλονίκι,
πήραν και την Αγιά Σοφιά, το μέγα μοναστήρι,
πόχει τρακόσια σήμαντρα κι εξήντα δυο καμπάνες·
κάθε καμπάνα και παπάς, κάθε παπάς και διάκος.
Σιμά να βγουν τα άγια κι ο βασιλεύς του κόσμου,
φωνή τούς ήλθε εξ ουρανού, αγγέλων απ' το στόμα:
«Αφήτε αυτήν την ψαλμωδιά, να χαμηλώσουν τ' άγια,
και στείλτε λόγον στη Φραγκιά, να 'λθουν να τα πιάσουν,
να πάρουν τον χρυσό σταυρό και τ' αργυρό ευαγγέλιο,
να πάρουν την αγίαν τράπεζα, να μην την αμολύνουν».
Σαν τ' άκουσε η Δέσποινα, δακρύζουν οι εικόνες.
«Σώπα, κυρία Δέσποινα, μην κλαίεις, μην δακρύζεις,
πάλε με χρόνους με καιρούς, πάλε δικά σου είναι».

The Sack of Constantinople

They've taken the City, taken her, taken Thessaloniki.
They've taken Agia Sofia too, the mighty monastery,
which had three hundred bells of wood, sixty-two of metal;
for every bell there was a priest, for every priest a deacon.
The great procession was to begin, with the emperor of the world,
when from the heavens a voice came down, from the angels' mouths:
'Leave off the chanting, leave it off, take down the holy objects,
and send word to the Frankish West to take them all away.
Let them take the golden cross, take the silver gospel,
and let them take the altar too, that it not be sullied.'
When Mother Mary heard that voice, the icons started weeping.
'Be still, Mary, Mother of God, stay your crying and weeping,
for once more in time and times, they'll be yours once more.'

This song refers to the sack of Constantinople (Istanbul), here simply called
the City, by the Ottoman Turks (1453), following their capture of Thessaloniki
(1422–30). According to tradition, the final liturgy in the great church of Agia
Sofia was interrupted just before the city's last emperor, Constantine Paleolo-
gus, began the service. The first part of the song borrows phraseology from the
laments for the dead.

Ο Βαρλάμης

Τρία πλάτανα, τα τρία αράδ᾽ αράδα,
κι ένας πλάτανος, παχύν ίσκιον οπόχει·
στα κλωνάρια του σπαθιά ᾽ναι κρεμασμένα
και στη ρίζα του ντουφέκια ακουμπισμένα,
κι αποκάτω του Βαρλάμης ξαπλωμένος.

Song of Varlamis

Three plane trees, three all in a row,
and one plane tree with deep, thick shadow;
in its branches swords are hanging,
at its foot are rifles leaning,
and underneath stretched out, reclining, lies Varlamis.

The identity of the brigand-hero of this song—which may be an extract from a longer, lost song—is unknown. The song has an unusual metre (which I have not replicated in the translation) and this may point to an early date for the song compared to the other songs of brigands.

Του Μπουκοβάλα

Το τι 'ν' αχός που γίνεται και ταραχή μεγάλη·
μηνά βουβάλια σφάζονται, μηνά θηριά μαλώνουν;
Κι ουδέ βουβάλια σφάζονται, κι ουδέ θηριά μαλώνουν·
ο Μπουκοβάλας πολεμά με χίλιους πεντακόσιους,
στη μέση του Κεράσοβου και στην Καινούρια Χώρα.
Ξανθή κόρη εχούιαξεν από το παραθύρι:
«Πάψε, Ιάννη μ', τον πόλεμο, πάψε και τα τουφέκια,
να κατακάτσει ο κονιορκτός, να σηκωθεί η αντάρα,
να μετρηθεί τ' ασκέρι σου, να ιδούμε πόσοι λείπουν».
Μετρούνται Τούρκοι τρεις βολές και λείπουν πεντακόσιοι·
μετρούνται τα κλεφτόπουλα και λείπουν δυο νομάτοι·
ο Δήμος ο πρωτόγερος κι ο Ιάννης ο Ψαλλίδας.

Song of Boukovalas

What is that sound that rings so loud, what is the great disturbance?
Is it wild beasts tussling, is it buffaloes butchered?
It's not wild beasts tussling, it's not buffaloes butchered;
it's Boukovalas making war, against fifteen hundred,
in the middle of Kerasovo, and in Kenourgia Chora.
Then from a window up above came a blonde girl's cry,
'O Yanni stop, O stop your war, stop your rifles firing,
and let the dust fall to the ground, let the black fog lift,
and let us count your band of men, let us count up the missing.'
They count the Turks three times, five hundred men are missing.
They count their own brigand lads, and only two are missing—
Dimos the first dignitary and Yannis Psalidas.

Yannis Boukovalas was born around 1700 and became one of the most famous captains of the mountainous Agrafa region of Central Greece. He was such a renowned brigand that at one time the brigand songs in their entirety were called the 'Boukovaleika'. One of the few pieces of information we have about him is that he fought against the forebears of Ali Pasha. As with many of the brigand songs, however, the specific battle cannot be identified.

Του Ζίντρου

Ζίντρο μου, ήσουν φρόνιμος απ' όλα τα πρωτάτα,
ήσουν και πρώτος έξαρχος σ' όλα τα μοναστήρια.
Όσα βουνά θέλεις διαβεί και κάμπους ν' απεράσεις,
όλα βοτάνια έχουνε κι όλα βοτάνια κάμνουν.
Να τά 'ξευρες, να τά 'τρωγες, ποτέ να μην πεθάνεις.
«Τι σήμερο και τι ταχύ, 'γώ ν' αποθάνω θέλω.
Δεν τό 'χω πως θενά χαθώ και πως θεν' αποθάνω,
μόν' τό 'χω σε παράπονο και σε ντροπή μεγάλη,
που θενά μπει Αρβανιτιά μέσα στην Ελασσόνα,
και θα μου κάψουν τα χωριά κι όλα τα βιλαέτια,
και θα το έχω σε ντροπήν, όπ' ήμουν καπετάνος».

Song of Zidros

Zidros, O Zidros, you were shrewd among all the captaincies,
you were the noble governor of all the monasteries.
All of the mountains that you cross, the fields that you pass over—
they all have herbs and healing plants—all have worts and balsams.
Oh that you knew them, oh that you ate them, never would you die.
'Today, tomorrow, what of it, I'll be dead and gone,
but it's not that I'll be dead and gone, it's not that I will perish,
it's that I'll have a sore complaint, it's that I'll be ashamed—
I'll be ashamed an Albanian crew will fill my Elassona,
and that they'll burn my villages, they'll burn my vilayets,
and I will be consumed with shame, that I was once a captain.'

Zidros was a captain of Mount Olympus and the nearby town and district of
Elassona, and was famed as much for his wisdom and longevity as for his fighting skill. He reportedly held his captaincy from 1720–70, during which time
there was much fighting between the Greek captains and their rival Albanian
pass guards (who guarded strategic mountain passes). 'Vilayets' were adminis-
trative provinces of the Ottoman Empire.

Του Νικοτσάρα

Ο Νικοτσάρας πολεμά με τρία βιλαέτια,
την Ζίχναν και τον Χάντακα, το έρημο το Πράβι.
Τρεις μέρες κάμνει πόλεμον, τρεις μέρες και τρεις νύχτες·
χιόν' έτρωγαν, χιόν' έπιναν και την φωτιά βαστούσαν.
Τα παλικάρια φώναξε στες τέσσαρες ο Νίκος:
«Ακούστε, παλικάρια μου, ολίγα κι αντρειωμένα,
σίδηρον βάλτε στην καρδιά, και χάλκωμα στα στήθη,
αύριον πόλεμον κακόν έχομεν με τους Τούρκους,
αύριον να πατήσομεν, να πάρομε το Πράβι».
Τον δρόμον πήραν σύνταχα κι έφθασαν στο γεφύρι,
ο Νίκος με το δαμασκί την άλυσόν του κόφτει·
φεύγουν οι Τούρκοι σαν τραγιά, πίσω το Πράβ' αφήνουν.

Song of Nikotsaras

Nikotsaras is making war with three vilayets:
with Zichna and with Handaka and with sad Pravi.
Three days long the battle goes, three days and nights it rages,
with snow to eat and snow to drink, never lighting a fire.
Then on the fourth day Nikos cries to all his fine young men,
'Listen lads and listen well, you're brave though few in number:
It's time to arm your chests with bronze, clad your hearts with iron,
for tomorrow there's a fierce fight to be done against the Turks.
Tomorrow it is we'll trample them, tomorrow Pravi is ours.'
At dawn they took the road, at dawn they reached the bridge,
and with his axe of Damascus steel Nikos cuts the chain:
the Turks scatter like billy goats, leaving Pravi behind them.

Nikotsaras (Nikos Tsaras), born around 1770, was the next-but-one successor
to Zidros as captain of Mount Olympus. He took on the captaincy but then
abandoned it for a life of piracy and banditry. The song refers to an expedition
undertaken by the brigand to join up with Russian forces in Romania and
provide assistance in the Russo-Turkish War (1806–12). He was urged on per-
sonally by the admiral Dmitry Senyavin, but never made it. Held up at Pravi
(now Eleftheroupoli, Eastern Macedonia), where the battle in the song
occurred, he broke through the resistance only to be killed several days later
on a raid of another village.

Ο Πλιάτσκας

Κείτεται ο Πλιάτσκας, κείτεται, κείτεται λαβωμένος,
με τα ποδάρια στο νερό, πάλε νερό χαλεύει.
«Νά 'χα νερό απ' τον τόπο μου και μήλ' απ' τη μηλιά μου,
νά 'χα και τη μανούλα μου, να πλένει τους γιαράδες,
να πλένει τες λαβωματιές, οπού 'μαι λαβωμένος».
Με τα πουλιά εμάλωνε και με τα χελιδόνια:
«Τάχα, πουλιά μ', θα γιατρευτώ, τάχα, πουλιά μ', θα γιάνω;»
«Πλιάτσκα μου, σα θέλεις γιατρειά, σα θέλεις να γερέψεις,
να βγεις απάνω στ' Άγραφα, ψηλά στ' αγραφοβούνια,
πού 'ναι τα κρύα τα νερά, και τα όμορφα κορίτσια».

Song of Pliatskas

There lies Pliatskas, there he lies, there he's lying wounded.
His legs in water dangling, yet still he calls for water.
'Oh had I water from my land, apples from my orchard,
Oh had I but my mother here, to wash and tend these wounds,
to wash these gashes, wash them well, everywhere I'm wounded.'
Then he conversed with the birds, debated with the swallows,
'Birds, sweet birds, will I be healed? Birds, will I get better?'
'Pliatskas, if you want to heal, if you want to get better,
go up to Agrafa, head to those high mountains.
It's there you'll find the lovely girls, it's there you'll find cool waters.'

Pliatskas was a contemporary of Nikotsaras and lived around Mount Olympus.
Given that most other variants of the song refer to Olympus, the last two lines
of this variant show how easily the songs could take on a different local flavour.
There are also noticeable echoes of the songs of Greeks far from home.

Ο Κίτσος και η μητέρα του

Του Κίτσ' η μάνα κάθουνταν 'πό πέρ' απ' το ποτάμι,
με το ποτάμι μάλωνε και το πετροβολούσε.
«Ποτάμι μ', γιά λιγόστεψε, ποτάμι μ', στρέψε πίσω,
για να περάσω αντίπερα, πέρα στα κλεφτοχώρια,
πόχουν οι κλέφτες σύνοδο, και παν στο συναγώγι».
Τον Κίτσο τον επιάσανε και παν να τον κρεμάσουν,
χίλιοι παγαίνουν εμπροσθά και χίλιοι από πίσω,
κι ολοξοπίσω πάγαινε, πηγαίνει κι η μανά του,
μοιριολογούσε κι έλεγε, μοιριολογά και λέγει·
«Κίτσο μου, πού 'ναι τ' άρματα, τα έρημα τσαπράζια;»
«Μάνα λωλή, μάνα ζουρλή, μάνα ξεμυαλισμένη,
μάνα μ', δεν κλαις τα νιάτα μου, και την παλικαριά μου,
μόν' κλαις τά 'ρημα τ' άρματα, τα έρημα τσαπράζια».

Kitsos and His Mother

Kitsos' mother she was sat on the river bank,
and she was quarrelling with that stream and pelting it with stones:
'River, won't you dry up for me; river, won't you turn back,
so I can cross to the other side, to the brigand villages,
where the brigands hold their meets, where they have their lairs?'
Kitsos was captured, he was seized, they took him off to hang him.
A thousand men went out in front, a thousand more behind him
and at the back, the very back, walked Kitsos' mother.
And she was singing a lament, and she was singing sadly,
'Kitsos, where are your weapons, where is your gleaming waistcoat?'
'Crazy mother, hare-brained mother; Mother, you've lost your wits!
Why don't you weep for my lost youth, for my graceful swagger,
but only for my wretched arms, and for my wretched waistcoat?'

The identity of Kitsos is unknown, as is the location of the river—perhaps
deliberately so, to shift the focus of the song from a specific brigand to brig-
andage in general.

Της Δέσπως – Πόλεμοι του Σουλίου

Αχός βαρύς ακούεται, πολλά τουφέκια πέφτουν·
μήνα εις γάμον ρίχνονται, μήνα κι εις χαροκόπι;
Ουδέ σε γάμον ρίχνονται, ουδέ κι εις χαρακόπι·
η Δέσπω κάμνει πόλεμον, με νύμφες και μ' εγγόνια.
Αρβανιτιά την πλάκωσε στου Δημουλά τον πύργον.
«Γιώργαινα, ρίξε τ' άρματα, δεν είν' εδώ το Σούλι,
εδώ είσαι σκλάβα του πασά, σκλάβα των Αρβανίτων».
«Το Σούλι κι αν προσκύνησε, κι αν τούρκεψεν η Κιάφα,
η Δέσπ' αφέντες Λιάπηδες, δεν έκαμ', ουδέ κάμνει».
Δαυλί στο χέρι άρπαξε, κόρες και νύμφες κράζει:
«Σκλάβες Τουρκών μη ζήσομεν, παιδιά, μαζί μ' ελάτε».
Και τα φυσέκια άναψε, κι όλοι φωτιά γενήκαν.

Song of Despo—the Souliote Wars

A crashing sound echoes around, musket volleys firing.
Are they firing at a wedding or at some festival?
They're not firing at a wedding, nor at some festival;
it's Despo who is making war, with daughters and granddaughters.
The Arvanites have hemmed her in, she's in Dimoula's tower.
'Put down your arms, little Yorgena, this isn't Souli here.
Here you are the Pasha's slave, slave of the Arvanites.'
'If Souli came to bow its head, if Kiafa turned Turk,
Albanians aren't Despo's lords, nor will they ever be.'
A torch she seizes in her hand, cries to the girls and women,
'Slaves of the Turks we'll never be—children, come beside me!'
And then she lit the cartridges, they all went up in flames.

This song refers to an episode at the end of the wars fought by Ali Pasha against
the people of the mountain region of Souli. Here, in December 1803, Despo
—wife of a certain Yorgi Botsis, hence her name 'Yorgena'—takes a last stand
against Ali Pasha's Arvanites in the coastal village of Riniasa (now Elatia).
She had fled the mountains after the fall of the strongholds of Souli and Kiafa.

Του Διάκου

Τρεις περδικούλες κάθουνταν ψηλά στη Χαλκουμάτα,
μοιριολογούσαν κι έλεγαν, μοιριολογούν και λέγουν:
«Ν-ο Διάκος τι να γίνηκε φέτο το καλοκαίρι;
Ν-ουδέ στην Πέτρα φάνηκε, ν-ουδέ στην Αταλάντη·
μας είπαν πως επέρασε πέρα στην Αλαμάνα,
να καρτερέσει τον πασιά κι αυτόν τον 'Μέρ Βρυώνη».
Κι Ομέρ Βρυώνης έφτασε με δώδεκα χιλιάδες
κι εκεί γράμματα τού 'στειλεν αυτός Ομέρ Βρυώνης:
«Έβγα, Διάκο μ', μη στέκεσαι και πιάσε τη Λαμία».
Κι αυτός ο μαύρος τού 'λεγε κι αυτός ο μαύρος λέγει:
«Ν-εγώ δεν είμαι νιόνυφη να πιάσω τη Λαμία·
ν-εγώ 'μαι Διάκος τρομερός με οχτακόσ' νουμάτοι».
Και πιάστηκαν στον πόλεμο τρεις μέρες και τρεις νύχτες.
Τρία γιρούσια ν-έκαμε, τα τρί' αράδα αράδα,
βούλωσε το ντουφέκι του, τσακίσ'κε το σπαθί του·
πιάσαν το Διάκο ζωντανό, το Διάκο παλικάρι.
Στη μέσ' Τούρκοι τον έβαλαν και τον βαριουξετάζουν:
«Γίνεσαι Τούρκος, Διάκο μου, την πίστη σου ν' αλλάξεις,
να προσκυνήσεις στο τζαμί, την εκκλησιά ν' αφήσεις;»
Κι αυτός ο μαύρος γέλαγε και στρίφτει το μουστάκι:
«Τί λέτ' αυτού, βρωμόσκυλα, σκυλιά μαγαρισμένα;
Εγώ Γραικός γεννήθηκα, Γραικός θεν' αποθάνω».
Και στο σουβλί τον έβαναν κι αυτός χαμογελάει.

Song of Athanasios Diakos

Three little partridges were perched high up at Halkoumata,
and they were singing a lament and they were singing sadly:
'What has become of Diakos? What happened to him this summer?
He didn't appear at Petra, nor at Atalanti,
and we've been told that he went over to Alamana,
lying in wait for the pasha, for that Omer Vrioni.'
And Omer Vrioni arrived just then, he had twelve thousand with him,
and to Diakos he sent word, to Diakos sent a letter;
'Diakos, good fellow, don't dally here—take shelter in Lamia.'
And that ill-fated man replied,
'I am no piddling young bride, to be sheltering in Lamia,
I am Diakos the terrible, and I've eight hundred with me'.
So then it was they fought a fight, three days and three nights long.
Diakos made three sallies, three all in a row,
and on the third his rifle jammed, his sword broke in his hand.
And so they took Diakos alive, they took that fine young man.
The Turks brought him to the square, made their inquisition:
'Become a Turk, Diakos—won't you change your faith,
won't you come to pray at the mosque, won't you leave the church?'
And that ill-fated man laughed, twirling his moustache:
'What are you saying you dirty dogs, you rotten, mangy dogs?
It's a Greek that I was born—and as a Greek will perish.'
So they roasted him on a spit, and he just keeps on smiling.

Athanasios Diakos was a hero of the Greek War of Independence. He was
impaled by the Ottoman Turks on 24 April 1821, while defending the Alamana
Bridge near Lamia. A lament is associated with his death (see p. 169).

Αιχμαλωσία του Κιαμίλ-Μπεη

Πήραν τα κάστρα, πήραν τα, πήραν και τα δερβένια,
πήραν και την Τριπολιτσάν, την ξακουσμένην χώραν.
Κλαίουν στους δρόμους Τούρκισσες, πολλές εμιροπούλες,
κλαίει και μια χανούμισσα τον δόλιον τον Κιαμίλην·
«Πού είσαι και δεν φαίνεσαι, καμαρωμέν' αφέντη;
Ήσουν κολόνα στον Μορεάν και φλάμπουρον στην Κόρθον,
ήσουν και στην Τριπολιτσάν πύργος θεμελιωμένος.
Στην Κόρθον πλεά δεν φαίνεσαι, ουδέ εις τα σαράια,
ένας παπάς τα έκαψε τα δόλια σου παλάτια».
Κλαίουν τ' αχούρια γι' άλογα και τα τζαμιά γι' αγάδες,
κλαίει και η Κιαμίλαινα τον δόλιον της τον άνδρα.
Σκλάβος ραϊάδων έπεσε, και ζει ραϊάς εκείνων.

The Capture of Kiamil-Bey

They've taken the castles, taken them, taken all the passes.
Tripolitsa is taken too—that place of fame far-reaching.
Turkish girls weep in the streets, those lovely Turkish beauties,
and one woman of the harem is weeping for poor Kiamil:
'Treasured master, where have you gone, won't you show yourself?
For you were Corinth's very flag, pillar of the Morea,
you were a fortress on your own—Tripolitsa's own stronghold.
Now in Corinth you don't appear, you do not grace your mansions,
and a priest has burned your wretched palaces.'
Stables are weeping for their steeds, mosques weep for their aghas,
and Kiamil's wife she's weeping too, for her poor, captured husband.
He's fallen slave to his own slaves, he's subject to his subjects.

The siege and capture of Tripolitsa (modern-day Tripoli, in the Peloponnese—here called the Morea) in 1821 was a decisive early victory for the
Greeks in the War of Independence and a massacre that attracted unfavourable
views abroad. Kiamil-bey, a wealthy Ottoman ruler based in the town of
Corinth, was captured during the siege and later killed. It is striking how this
lament is told from the point of view of the Greeks' enemies—the Turks.

Έξοδος του Μεσολογγίου

Σαββάτο μέρα πέρασα κοντά στο Μεσολόγγι·
ήτο Σαββάτο των Βαγιών, Σαββάτο του Λαζάρου,
κι άκουσα μαύρα κλιάματα, ανδρίκεια μοιρολόγια.
Δεν κλαίουν για το σκοτωμό, δεν κλαιν που θα πεθάνουν,
μόν' κλαιν που σώσαν το ψωμί, τους έφαγεν η πείνα.
Στην εκκλησιά συνάχτηκαν, μέσα στο άγιο Βήμα,
κι ένας τον άλλον έλεγαν, κι ένας τον άλλον λέγουν:
«Παιδιά, να μεταλάβομε, να ξιμολοηθούμε,
βράδυ γιουρούσ' θα κάμομε στα έξω για να βγούμε».

The Sortie from Mesolonghi

On Saturday I chanced to pass close to Mesolonghi,
and it was Lazarus' day, the day before Palm Sunday,
and there I heard the mournful cries, I heard brave men lamenting.
They weren't crying for the bloodshed, that they were going to die,
but that their bread had been used up, hunger had consumed them.
And they conferred inside the church, within the very chancel,
and one said to the other, they said amongst themselves,
'Friends, let's take communion; friends, let's make confession,
tonight we'll make a dash for it, we'll make our break for freedom.'

The heroic sortie from the town of Mesolonghi on 22 April 1826—a significant
event in the Greek War of Independence—was intended to break the year-long
Ottoman siege and bring the inhabitants to safety. In the event, almost every-
one was killed.

Ο θάνατος του Καραϊσκάκη

Τρεις περδικούλες κάθονταν στο κάστρο της Αθήνας,
είχαν τα νύχια κόκκινα και τα φτερά βαμμένα,
είχαν και τα κεφάλια τους στο αίμα βουτημένα.
Μοιρολογούσαν κι έλεγαν, μοιρολογούν και λένε:
«Τρίτη, Τετάρτη χλιβερή, Πέφτη φαρμακωμένη,
Παρασκευή ξημέρωσε, μην έχει ξημερώσει,
που πιάστηκε ο πόλεμος, το Κρητικό ντουφέκι».
Καραϊσκάκης τ' άκουσε, ήταν και θερμασμένος,
και τον σεΐζη του έκραξε και του σεΐζη λέγει:
«Σεΐζη, φκιάσε τ' άλογο, βάλ' του και το τακίμι,
κρίν' τε και των συντρόφων μας των καπεταναραίων·
να βγούμ' να πολεμήσουμε στον κάμπο της Αθήνας».
Σαν πιάστηκε ο πόλεμος, σκοτίστηκε ο κάμπος,
βαρέθηκε ο αρχηγός και ο Καραϊσκάκης:
«Παιδιά μ', να νταγιαντίσετε, να γίνετ' ένα σώμα,
να μη χαθεί η πατρίδα μας, την πάρτε στο λαιμό σας.
Μένα με παν στην Κούλουρη, πέρα στον Αϊ-Δημήτρη,
που είναι παντοτινός γιατρός, αυτός θα με γιατρέψει».
Πουλάκι πήγε κι έκατσε στου Αϊ-Δημητριού το δέντρο,
δεν ελαλούσε σαν πουλί, ουδέ σα χελιδόνι,
μόν' το δεντρί μαράθηκε απ' τον κελαηδισμό του.
Τον κλαίνε χώρες και χωριά κι όλ' οι καπεταναίοι,
τον κλαιν τα παλικάρια του κι όλος ο ταϊφάς του.

The Death of Karaiskakis

Three little partridges were perched on the citadel of Athens,
their claws were painted red, their wings were steeped in red,
and reddened were their little heads—they were dipped in blood.
And they were singing a lament, and they were singing sadly,
'Tuesday, Wednesday full of sorrow; bitter, poisoned Thursday;
then it was that Friday dawned—but oh that it had not! —
when war broke out, the fight began, the Cretan musket sounded.'
Karaiskakis heard those words, and he got in a fury,
and summoning his groom he cries,
'Groom, saddle my horse, give it all its trappings!
Send word to our companions, send word to all the captains,
that we'll be going out to fight on the plain of Athens.'
When battle was joined on that day, the plain darkened over,
a bullet struck the general, wounded Karaiskakis:
'Lads, hold out; lads, endure; lads, become one body,
and see to it yourselves that our land will not be lost.
They're taking me to Koulouri, the church of St Dimitris;
the saint was always my physician, and he will make me better.'
A little bird sat on a tree at St Dimitris' church;
its song was nothing like a bird's, it didn't sing like a swallow,
but when the bird sang its song, the tree dried up and withered.
Now the captains are all mourning him, the villages and the lands,
and his fine men are mourning too, his men and all his band.

This song honours the death of Georgios Karaiskakis, hero of the Greek Revolution, during the Ottoman siege of the Acropolis (1826–27), in a skirmish purportedly started by a group of (drunk) Cretans. The song was first sung by General Makriyannis, also present at the battle, and recorded in his memoirs.

BALLADS

The ballads are long, narrative poems that typically depict extreme, often violent domestic dramas in a gruesomely realistic way. They were recited rather than sung, and hence have been referred to as 'table' songs (*tis tavlas*) as opposed to dance songs. The origin of the ballads' beguiling Greek name —*paraloges*—has been debated over the last century. The most persuasive theory traces its etymology to the ancient Greek word *parakatalogi* (παρακαταλογή), meaning 'recitative'. It is possible that the form of the ballads has its roots in a kind of theatre that flourished in late antiquity after the demise of classical drama. These pantomime-like plays, acted by one person, often drew on classical mythology for their subjects. Here I have combined several *paraloges* with two songs usually classed as 'Akritic' (the final two in the section). The term Akritic refers to heroic medieval songs, prevalent in the eastern part of the old Greek world (from the Aegean islands to what is now eastern Turkey) and dating back to the frontier wars between the Byzantine Empire and the early Islamic world (seventh to eleventh centuries CE).

Του νεκρού αδερφού

Μάνα με τους εννιά τους γιους και με τη μια σου κόρη,
την κόρη τη μονάκριβη, την πολυαγαπημένη,
την είχες δώδεκα χρονώ κι ο ήλιος δεν την είδε·
στα σκοτεινά την έλουζες, στ' άφεγγα την επλέκας,
στ' άστρα και στον αυγερινό έφκιανες τα σγουρά της.
Οπού σε φέραν προξενιά από τη Βαβυλώνα
να την παντρέψεις στα μακριά, πολύ μακριά στα ξένα.
Οχτώ αδελφοί δε θέλουνε κί Κωσταντίνος θέλει.

«Δώσ' τηνε μάνα, δώσ' τηνε την Αρετή στα ξένα,
στα ξένα κει που περπατώ, στα ξένα που παγαίνω,
να 'χω κι εγώ παρηγοριά, να 'χω κι εγώ κονάκι».
«Φρόνιμος είσαι, Κωσταντή, κι άσχημ' απελογήθης·
κι αν μ' έρθει, γιε μου, θάνατος, κι αν μ' έρθει, γιε μ', αρρώστια,
κι αν τύχει πίκρα γιά χαρά, ποιος θα με τηνε φέρει;»

Τον Θεό τής έβαλ' εγγυτή και τους αγιούς μαρτύρους,
αν τύχει κι έρθει θάνατος, αν τύχει κι έρθει αρρώστια,
κι αν τύχει πίκρα γιά χαρά, να πάει να τη φέρει.
Και σαν την επαντρέψανε την Αρετή στα ξένα,
και μπήκε χρόνος δίσεκτος και μήνες οργισμένοι,
κι έπεσε το θανατικό κι οι εννιά αδελφοί πεθάναν,
βρέθηκ' η μάνα μοναχή, σαν καλαμιά στον κάμπο.
Παιδάκια κοιλοπόνεσε, παιδιά δεν έχ' κοντά της·
χορτάριασε η πόρτα της, πρασίνισε κι η αυλή της.

The Ballad of the Dead Brother

Mother with your nine sons and with your only daughter,
that precious only daughter, the one you loved so dearly,
twelve years old and you kept her in—the sun it never saw her,
you washed her in the hours of night, braided her hair in the darkness;
under the stars, the morning star, you fixed her lovely tresses.
And then matchmakers arrived from far-off Babylon,
seeking her in marriage there, in distant foreign lands.
Eight of the brothers didn't want the match, but Constantine he wanted.

'Give her, mother, give Areti, send her off abroad,
so in the strange lands where I go, the strange lands where I travel,
I'll have a place to lay my head, I'll have some consolation.'
'Constantine, from one so shrewd, these are ugly words.
Son, what if death should come to me; son, what if illness comes?
If joy or sorrow chance to come, who'll bring her back to me?'

He set God as his guarantor, the saints as witnesses,
if death should chance to come to her, if illness come upon her,
or joy or sorrow chance to come, he'd bring her back to Mother.
And when they'd married Areti in those far-distant lands,
and years came full of woe and months came wrathfully,
and death fell on the land and those nine sons were taken,
the mother was left abandoned, like the stubble of the field.
She'd borne her babes in pain, she now had none beside her.
Moss had sprouted on her door, her courtyard was grassed over.

Στα οχτώ μνήματα δέρνεται, στα οχτώ μοιρολογάει,
στου Κωσταντίνου το θαφτό τις πλάκες ανασκώνει.

«Σήκω, Κωσταντινάκη μου, την Αρετή μου θέλω·
τον Θεό μού 'βαλες εγγυτή και τους αγιούς μαρτύρους,
αν τύχει πίκρα για χαρά, να πας να με τη φέρεις».

Ο Κωσταντής ταράχθηκε 'πό μέσα το μνημόρι·
κάνει το σύννεφ' άλογο και τ' άστρο σαλιβάρι,
και το φεγγάρι συντροφιά και πάγει να τη φέρει.
Παίρνει τα όρη πίσω του και τα βουνά μπροστά του,
βρίσκει την και χτενίζουνταν έξω στο φεγγαράκι.
Από μακριά τη χαιρετά κι από μακριά της λέγει:

«Περπάτησ', Αρετούλα μου, κι η μάνα μας σε θέλει».
«Αλίμονο, αδελφάκι μου, και τι είν' τούτ' η ώρα;
Αν είναι ίσως για χαρά, να βάλω τα χρυσά μου,
κι αν είναι πίκρα, πες με το, να 'ρθω καταπώς είμαι».
«Περπάτησ', Αρετούλα μου, κι έλα καταπώς είσαι».

Στη στράτα που διαβαίνανε, στη στράτα που πηγαίναν,
ακούν πουλιά να κελαηδούν, ακούν πουλιά να λένε:
«Ποιος είδε κόρην όμορφη να σέρν' αποθαμένος;»
«Άκουσες, Κωσταντάκη μου, τι λένε τα πουλάκια;
"Ποιος είδε κόρην όμορφη να σέρν' αποθαμένος"!»
«Λωλά πουλιά κι ας κελαηδούν, λωλά πουλιά κι ας λένε».
«Τι βλέπουμε τα θλιβερά, τα παραπονεμένα,
να περπατούν οι ζωντανοί με τους αποθαμένους!»

On eight tombs she beat her hands, on eight she lamented,
and on the grave of Constantine she raised the slab.

'Get up, young Constantine, I want my daughter back.
You set God as your guarantor, the saints as witnesses,
if joy or sorrow chance to come, you'd bring her back to me.'

From deep within his tomb Constantine was shaken.
And of a cloud he makes his horse, of the stars he makes its reins,
and with the moon for company he goes to bring her back.
Mountains he leaps in front of him, leaves mountains in his wake,
finds Areti combing her locks outside under the moonlight.
And from afar he greets her and from afar he says,

'Walk with me, Areti, our mother wants you back.'
'O brother, what is it at this hour?
If it's for joy, tell me so, I'll put on all my gold;
if it's for sorrow, tell me so, I'll come just as I am.'
'Walk with me, Areti, and come just as you are.'

And as they went along their path, as they went their way,
they hear the song of little birds, hear them as they say,
'Whoever saw so fair a girl walking with a corpse?'
'Did you hear, Constantine, what the birds are saying?
—Whoever saw so fair a girl walking with a corpse?'
'The birds are mad, so let them sing; so let the mad birds speak.'
'What's this we see, we sad, sad birds, we sorrowful little birds?
The living walking hand in hand with the dead departed!'

«Άκουσες, Κωσταντάκη μου, τι λένε τα πουλάκια;
Πως περπατούν οι ζωντανοί με τους αποθαμένους».
«Πουλάκια είν' κι ας κελαηδούν, πουλάκια είν' κι ας λένε».
«Φοβούμαι σε, αδελφάκι μου, και λιβανιές μυρίζεις».
«Εχτές βραδύ επήγαμε πέρα στον Άι-Γιάννη,
και θύμιασέ μας ο παπάς με περισσό λιβάνι».

Και παραμπρός που πήγαιναν κι άλλα πουλιά τούς λένε·
«Θεέ μεγαλοδύναμε, μεγάλο θάμα κάνεις,
τέτοια πανώρια λυγερή να σέρν' αποθαμένος».

Τ' άκουσε πάλ' η λυγερή και ράγισ' η καρδιά της.
«Άκουσες, Κωσταντάκη μου, τι λένε τα πουλάκια;
Πες με πού 'ν' τα μαλλάκια σου, το πηγουρό μουστάκι;»
«Μεγάλ' αρρώστια μ' έβρηκε, μ' έριξε του θανάτου,
με πέσαν τα ξανθιά μαλλιά, το πηγουρό μουστάκι».

Βρίσκουν το σπίτι κλειδωτό, κλειδομανταλωμένο,
και τα σπιτοπαράθυρα πού 'ταν αραχνιασμένα.

«Άνοιξε, μάνα μ', άνοιξε και νά την η Αρετή σου».
«Αν είσαι Χάρος διάβαινε κι άλλα παιδιά δεν έχω·
και μέν' η Αρετούλα μου λείπ' μακριά στα ξένα».
«Άνοιξε, μάνα μ', άνοιξε κι εγώ είμ' ο Κωσταντής σου·
εγγυτή σου 'βαλα τον Θεό και τους αγιούς μαρτύρους,
αν τύχει πίκρα για χαρά, να πάω να σε τη φέρω».

Ώσπου να βγει στην πόρτα της, εβγήκε η ψυχή της.

'Did you hear, Constantine, what the birds are saying?
—The living walking hand in hand with the dead departed!'
'They're just birds, so let them sing; let them babble on.'
'Brother, I am scared of you, you're reeking strong of incense.'
'Sister, it was yesternight we went to St John's chapel,
and the priest censed us all with plenty of strong incense.'

And further on were other birds, speaking to them like this,
'Almighty and all-powerful God, what a miracle you're working,
that such a fair and lovely girl is walking with a corpse.'

The lovely girl heard again; her heart shivered within her.
'Did you hear, Constantine, what the birds are saying?
So tell me, where's your hair, where is your thick moustache?'
'A great sickness crippled me, put me at death's door,
and all my yellow locks fell out, and my thick moustache.'

They find the house closed up, locked and iron-barred,
and all the windows of the house were spider-black and cobwebbed.

'Open, Mother, open up, your Areti is here.'
'If you're Charos, go on by, I have no other children,
and only Areti is left, and she's in foreign parts.'
'Open, Mother, open up, your Constantine is here.
I set God as my guarantor, the saints as witnesses
if joy or sorrow chance to come, I'd bring her back to you.'

Before the mother reached the door, her soul had flown away.

Τα κακά πεθερικά

Ο Κωσταντίνος ο μικρός κι ο μικροπαντρεμένος
το Μάη φυτιάν εφύτεψε, το Μάη γυναίκα πήρε,
το Μάη τού 'ρθε μήνυμα να πάει στο σεφέρι,
και το σεφέρι του μακρύ κι η ρόγα του 'ναι λίγη·
τον παραστέκ' η κόρη του και στεφανωτικιά του:
«Μισεύεις, Κωσταντάκη μου; Κι εμένα πού μ' αφήνεις;»
«Πρώτα σ' αφήνω στον Θεό και δεύτερα στσ' Αγίους
και τρίτα στη μανούλα μου, στα δυο γλυκά μ' αδέρφια».

Μητ' ένα μίλι λείπ' ο νιος μητ' ένα μήτε δύο,
στο σκάνιο την εβάλανε και την τριχοκουρέψαν,
της κόψαν τα ξανθά μαλλιά, την όμορφη πλεξίδα,
της δίνουν γιδοπρόβατα κι εκείνα ψωριασμένα,
της δίνουνε κι ένα σκυλί κι εκείνο λυσσασμένο,
της δίνουνε και τριά ψωμιά κι εκείνα μουχλιασμένα,
κι από το χέρι την κρατούν, και τσ' άμοιρης τση λένε:

«Θωρείς εκείνο το βουνό το βαρυχιονισμένο;
Εκεί θα πας να βραδιαστείς κι εκεί να κατοικήσεις,
κι αν δεν χιλιάσεις πρόβατα κι αν δεν μυριάσεις γίδια,
στον κάμπο να μην κατεβείς να τα περιβοσκήσεις,
και στο ποτάμι μην ερθείς να τα περιποτίσεις».

Παίρνει τη στράτα η ορφανή, παίρνει το μονοπάτι,
κι ως τό 'θελεν η μοίρα της, τ' ωριό το ριζικό της,
τ' αρνί τσ' αρνί της γέννουνε κι η προβατίνα πέντε,

The Wicked In-laws

There was a young man, Constantine, and he was married young.
In May he planted in the ground, in May he took a woman,
in May a message came to him to fight in the campaign,
and far, how far was the campaign—how little was his payment.
Next to him there stands his girl, the girl that he has married,
'You're off, my darling Constantine? Who will you leave me with?'
'It's first I'll leave you unto God, second unto the saints,
and third in my sweet mother's care, with both my darling brothers.'

The young man wasn't a mile away—not one nor even two,
when they rounded on the girl, they cut off all her hair.
They cut off all those lovely plaits, that blonde hair finely braided,
they gave her mangy sheep and goats,
gave her a rabid dog,
and finally they gave to her three bits of mouldy bread,
and then they grabbed her by the hand and said to that poor girl,

'You see that mountain over there, blanketed with snow?
It's there you'll spend the night, it's there you'll make a dwelling;
and if the sheep don't multiply, the goats don't number thousands,
don't think of coming to the plains to bring them there for pasture,
don't think of coming to the stream, to bring them there for water.'

That orphan-sad girl makes her way, takes the path before her,
and as her fortune wanted it, that lucky fate of hers,
her lambs gave birth to other lambs, each ewe gave birth to five,

κι εχίλιασε τα πρόβατα κι εμύριασε τα γίδια·
και σαν εχίλιασε τ' αρνιά κι εμύριασε τα γίδια,
περνάσαν χρόνοι και χρονιές και μήνες κι εβδομάδες,
στους κάμπους εκατέβηκε να τα περιβοσκήσει,
και στο νερό του ποταμού να τα περιποτίσει.

Νά σου κι ο Κώστας πού 'ρχονταν στον κάμπο καβαλάρης.
«Γεια σου, χαρά σου, πιστικέ» – «Καλώς το παλικάρι».
«Ποιανού 'ν' αυτά τα πρόβατα; Ποιανού 'ν' αυτά τα γίδια;»
«Τα πρόβατά 'ναι της βροντής, της αστραπής τα γίδια».
«Ποιανού κι ο χαϊδοπιστικός, πόχ' αηδονιού λαλίτσα;»
«Ο πιστικός που το βοσκεί του Κώστα η γυναίκα».
«Καλά το 'πε η καρδούλα μου, καλά το 'πε η καρδιά μου».

Βουτσιά δίνει του μαύρου του, στο σπίτι του παγαίνει.
«Γειά σου, χαρά σου μάνα μου» – «Καλώς το το παιδί μου».
«Μάνα, πού 'ν' η γυναίκα μου; Μάνα, πού 'ν' η καλή μου;»
«Παιδί μου κείνη πέθανε εδώ και τόσους χρόνους».
«Δείξε μου το μνημούρι της, να πάω να το συγκλάψω,
να βάλω κερολίβανο για το μνημόσυνό της».
«Εκείνο, γιε μου, χόρτιασε, και γνωρισμούς δεν έχει,
το πλάκωσε ξεραγκαθιά, το σκέπασε τσουκνίδα».
«Κι αν είν' ακόμα ζωντανή, τι θέλεις να σου κάνω;»
«Αν είν' ακόμα ζωντανή, κόβε μου το κεφάλι».

«Μάνα μ', άξια η κρίσις σου κι ο Θιός να σ' το πλερώσει».
Βουτσιά δίνει του μαύρου του, στον κάμπο κατεβαίνει,

and so her sheep multiplied, her goats numbered thousands.
And when the lambs had multiplied, the kids numbered thousands,
the years had come and gone, the months and weeks had passed,
the girl came to the plains, she brought her flocks for pasture,
she brought them to the stream, she brought them there for water.

And look! here comes our Constantine, riding across the plains.
'Greetings, shepherd, good day to you'—'Good day to you, fine sir.'
'Tell me, whose are the sheep you graze, who do the goats belong to?'
'Born of the thunder are the sheep, the goats are of the lightning.'
'And, pretty shepherd, who are you, with the voice of a nightingale?'
'The shepherd who is grazing them is wife of Constantine.'
'And so my little heart was right.'

He lashes onwards his black horse, onwards to his home.
'Greetings, Mother, good day to you'—'Good day to you, my son.'
'Tell me, Mother, where is my wife? Where is my good woman?'
'Child, your wife is dead and gone, it's years ago she perished.'
'Well then, Mother, show me her tomb, so I can weep for her,
and burn an incense candle, to cherish her memory.'
'Child, her tomb has weeded up, it can't be recognized,
the brambles have grown thick on it, it's overgrown with nettles.'
'And if I find that she's alive, what should I do to you?'
'Child, if you find that she's alive, you can cut off my head.'

'Mother, what you say is just—may God be witness to it!'
He lashes onwards his black horse, onwards to the plains,

κι ο μαύρος εγονάτισε κι η κόρ' απάνω βρέθη.
Πάλε βουτσιά τού βάρεσε, στο σπίτι του γυρίζει.

«Μάνά 'ν' την η γυναίκα μου, μάνά 'ν' την η καλή μου».
«Κώστα μου, σαν την εύρηκες, κόψε μου το κεφάλι».

his black horse stoops down on its knees, the girl gets upon it,
and lashing his horse again, he makes straightway for home.

'Mother, here is my wife, here is my good woman.'
'Since you found her, Constantine, go on—cut off my head!'

Ο γυρισμός του ξενιτεμένου

Ερόδισε γ-η ανατολή και ξημερώνει η δύση
γλυκοχαράζουν τα βουνά κι ο αυγερινός τραβιέται,
παν τα πουλάκια στη βοσκή κι οι λυγερές στη βρύση.
Βγαίνω κι εγώ κι ο μαύρος μου και τα λαγωνικά μου.
Βρίσκω μια κόρη πόπλενε σε μαρμαρένια γούρνα.
Τη χαιρετάω, δε μου μιλεί, της κρένω δε μου κρένει.

«Κόρη, γιά βγάλε μας νερό, την καλή μοίρα νά 'χεις,
να πιω κι εγώ κι ο μαύρος μου και τα λαγωνικά μου».

Σαράντα σίκλους έβγαλε, στα μάτια δεν την είδα,
κι απάνω στους σαρανταδυό τη βλέπω δακρυσμένη.

«Γιατί δακρύζεις, λυγερή, και βαριαναστενάζεις;
Μήνα πεινάς, μήνα διψάς, μην έχεις κακή μάνα;»
«Μήτε πεινώ, μήτε διψώ, μήτ' έχω κακή μάνα.
Ξένε μου, κι αν εδάκρυσα κι αν βαριαναστενάζω,
τον άντρα 'χω στην ξενιτιά και λείπει δέκα χρόνους,
κι ακόμη δυο τον καρτερώ, στους τρεις τον παντυχαίνω·
κι αν δεν ερθεί, κι α δε φανεί, καλόγρια θα γένω,
θα πάγω σ' έρημα βουνά, να στήσω μοναστήρι,
και στο κελί θα σφαλιστώ, στα μαύρα θελά βάψω,
εκειόν να τρώγει η ξενιτιά κι εμέ τα μαύρα ράσα».

«Κόρη μου, ο άντρας σου πέθανε, κόρη μου, ο άντρας σου χάθη.
Τα χέρια μου τον κράτησαν, τα χέρια μου τον θάψαν,

The Return of the Long-Lost Husband

The east was turning rosy red, in the west day was breaking,
over the mountains dawn came sweet, the morning star retreated,
the birds were winging to the plains, the girls to the fountain.
And I was out on my black horse and with my pack of hounds.
I met a girl washing clothes at the marble trough.
I greeted her, she didn't reply; I spoke, she didn't answer.

'Won't you give us some water, girl, and may your fate be happy;
so I can drink, my black horse too, and my pack of hounds.'

She drew out forty bucketfuls, I hadn't seen her eyes,
but on the forty-second one, I saw that she was weeping.

'Why are you weeping, lovely one, why is your heart so heavy?
Is it from hunger, is it from thirst, or is your mother wicked?'
'It's not from hunger, it's not from thirst, nor is my mother wicked.
If I am weeping, stranger, and if my heart is heavy,
it's for my husband who's abroad, who's been away ten years.
I'll wait for him another two, and on the third I'll meet him,
but if he doesn't come back then, I'll take a nun's black habit,
I'll go to the barren mountainsides, I'll found a nunnery,
I'll bolt myself inside a cell, I'll paint it black inside.
He'll waste away from being abroad, and I from my black habit.'

'My girl, your husband's died abroad, my girl, your husband's gone.
I held him with these very hands, with these hands he was buried.

ψωμί κερί τού μοίρασα κι είπε να τα πλερώσεις,
τον έδωκα κι ένα φιλί, κι είπε να μου το δώσεις».
«Ψωμί κερί τού μοίρασες, διπλά να σε πληρώσω,
μα για τ' εκείνο το φιλί, σύρε να σου το δώσει».

«Κόρη μου, εγώ είμαι ο άντρας σου, εγώ είμαι κι ο καλός σου».
«Ξένε μου, αν είσαι ο άντρας μου, αν είσαι κι ο καλός μου,
δείξε σημάδια της αυλής και τότε να πιστέψω».

«Έχεις μηλιά στην πόρτα σου και κλήμα στην αυλή σου,
κάνει σταφύλι ραζακί και το κρασί μοσκάτο,
κι όποιος το πιει δροσίζεται και πάλι αναζητά το».
«Αυτά είν' σημάδια της αυλής, τα ξέρει ο κόσμος όλος,
διαβάτης ήσουν, πέρασες, τα είδες και μου τα λέεις.
Πες μου σημάδια του σπιτιού και τότες να πιστέψω».

«Ανάμεσα στην κάμαρα χρυσό καντίλι ανάφτει,
και φέγγει σου, που γδύνεσαι και πλέκεις τα μαλλιά σου,
φέγγει σου τις γλυκές αυγές, που τα καλά σου βάζεις».
«Κάποιος κακός μου γείτονας σου τά 'πε και τα ξέρεις.
Πες μου σημάδια του κορμιού, σημάδια της αγάπης».

«Έχεις ελιά στα στήθη σου κι ελιά στην αμασκάλη,
κι ανάμεσα στα δυο βυζιά τ' αντρού σου φυλακτάρι».

«Ξένε μου, εσύ είσαι ο άντρας μου, εσύ είσαι κι ο καλός μου».

I shared bread and candles with him, he said you would repay me,
and when I gave a final kiss, he said you'd give it back.'
'If you shared bread and candles, I'll pay you back twice over,
but of that final kiss you gave, you'll have to get it from him.'

'But I am your good man, my girl; it's me that is your husband.'
'Stranger, if you are my good man, and if you are my husband,
tell me the signs of my courtyard—then I will believe you.'

'An apple tree stands at your gate, a vine grows in your courtyard,
and it produces rose-red grapes and they produce sweet muscat,
and those who drink it are refreshed and long for it again.'
'Those are the signs of the courtyard, and everybody knows them,
if you were a passer-by, you could have seen and told me.
Tell me the sure signs of the house and then I will believe you.'

'Inside your bedroom shines a light, a golden gleaming lamp,
it shines on you when you undress and when you braid your hair,
it shines on you on those sweet dawns when you put on your finest.'
'For you to know, you've sure been told by some wicked neighbour.
Tell me the signs on my body, tell me the signs of love.'

'There's a beauty spot on your breast, a mole under your arm,
and there, between your breasts, is your husband's amulet.'

'Stranger, it's you are my good man, it's you who are my husband.'

Η μάνα η φόνισσα

Ο Ανδρόνικος εκίνησε να πάει λαφοκυνήγι,
εκίνησε κι ο Κωσταντής στο δάσκαλο να πάει,
το καλαμάρι αστόχησε, γυρίζει να το πάρει.
Βρίσκει την πόρτα ν-ανοιχτή, την πόρτα ν-ανοιγμένη,
βρίσκει την μάνα του αγκαλιά με ξένο παλικάρι.
«Ας είναι, ας είναι, μάνα μου, κι α δε σ' ομολογήσω,
κι α δεν το πω τ' αφέντη μου, ν' άδικοθανατίσω».
«Τι είδες, μωρέ, και τι θα πεις και τι θα μολογήσεις;»
«Καλό είδα 'γώ, καλό θα ειπώ, καλό θα μολογήσω,
κακό είδα 'γώ, κακό θα ειπώ, κακό θα μολογήσω».

Και με το μόσκο το πλανά και με τα λεφτοκάρυα,
και στο κελάρι τό 'μπασε και σαν τ' αρνί το σφάζει,
σα μακελάρης φυσικός του βγάζει το συκώτι.
Σ' εννιά νερά το ξέπλυνε και ξεπλυμούς δεν είχε,
και πάλε το ξανάπλυνε και πάλι ν-αίμα στάζει·
και στο τηγάνι το 'βαλε για να το τηγανίσει.

Και νά σου κι ο Ανδρόνικος στους κάμπους καβαλάρης,
βροντομαχούν τα ρούχα του και λάμπουν τ' άρματά του,
φέρνει τα λάφια ζωντανά, τ' αγρίμια μερωμένα,
φέρνει κι ένα λαφόπουλο του Κωσταντή παιχνίδι.
Κοντοκρατεί το μαύρο του και τηνε χαιρετάει.
«Γεια σου, χαρά σου, ποθητή, και πού 'ναι ο Κωσταντής μας;»
«Τον έλουσα, τον άλλαξα, και στο σκολειό τον πήγα».
Φτερνιά δίνει τ' αλόγου του και στο σκολειό πηγαίνει.

Mother Murderess

Andronikos set forth one morning on a deer hunt,
and Constantine set forth too, to study with his master,
but he forgot his quill and ink, he went back home to fetch them.
He finds the front door open wide, the door is standing open,
he finds his mother in the arms of a young man, a stranger,
'So be it, Mother, so be it then, just see if I don't tell,
just see if I don't tell my father, so be it if I'm murdered.'
'What did you see, you little wretch, what do you have to tell?'
'If I saw good, I'll say it so—I will tell of good.
If I saw wrong, I'll say it so—I will tell of wrong.'

Then with musk she led him off, with musk and hazelnut,
and in a cell she shut him up, slaughtered him like a lamb,
and as a real butcher carves did she carve out his liver.
In nine waters she rinsed the blood, but it would not be rinsed.
Again she rinsed, again, again, and still the blood was dripping.
She threw it in a frying pan and set about to fry it.

And look! here comes Andronikos, riding across the plains,
his clothes are clanging loud as war, his armour glints,
he brings the deer alive, the wild beasts he's tamed,
he brings a little fawn for Constantine to play with.
And tethering his black horse he goes to greet his wife.
'Good day to you, beloved, but where's our Constantine?'
'I washed his hair, I changed his clothes and took him off to school.'
Onwards he spurs his black horse, onwards he makes for school.

«Δάσκαλε, πού 'ναι ο Κωσταντής και πού είναι το παιδί μου;»
«Δυο μέρες έχω να το ιδώ και τρεις να το διαβάσω».
Φτερνιά δίνει τ' αλόγου του, στο σπίτι του πηγαίνει.
«Γυναίκα, πού είναι ο Κωσταντής και πού είναι το παιδί μας;»
«Στης πεθεράς μου τό 'στειλα, κι όπου κι αν είναι θά 'ρθει».
Φτερνιά δίνει τ' αλόγου του, στης μάνας του πηγαίνει.
«Μάνα μου, πού είναι ο Κωσταντής και πού είναι το παιδί μου;»
«Έχω δυο μέρες να το ιδώ και τρεις να το φιλήσω,
κι α δεν το ιδώ ως το βραδύ θενά παραλοΐσω».
Φτερνιά δίνει τ' αλόγου του στο σπίτι του πηγαίνει.
«Σκύλα, και πού είν' ο Κωσταντής, ο μικροκωσταντίνος;»
«Κάπου παιγνίδι ν-εύρηκε και θελά παιγνιδίζει».
«Γυναίκα, βάλε μου να φάω, να φάω να γεματίσω,
να πάρω δίπλα τα βουνά, δίπλα τα καταράχια,
να πάω να βρω τον Κωσταντή, το φύτρο της καρδάς μου».

Το συκωτάκι τού 'βαλε σ' ένα ασημένιο πιάτο.
Πρώτη μπουκιά ν-οπού 'βαλε το συκωτάκι πήρε,
το συκωτάκι μίλησε, το συκωτάκι λέει.
«Αν είσαι σκύλος, φάε με, κι Οβριός απέταξέ με,
κι αν είσαι κι ο πατέρας μου, σκύψε και φίλησέ με».
Και την μπουκιά του απέλυσε, τρογύρω του κοιτάει,
εβούρκωσε η καρδούλα του, εμαύρισε το φως του,
τα δάκρυα τρέξαν ποταμός, κι εκόντεψε να πέσει.
Μα ν-αντρειώθη κι έσυρε το δαμασκί σπαθί του,
και στο λαιμό της τό 'βαλε, της κόβει το κεφάλι·
λιανά λιανά την έκοψε, στον ήλιο την απλώνει,
κι από τον ήλιο στο σακί, κι απ' το σακί στο μύλο.

'Master, where is my Constantine? Tell me—where is my son?'
'It's two days since I saw him last, three days since I taught him.'
Onwards he spurs his black horse, makes for home again.
'Woman, where is our Constantine? Woman, where is our son?'
'I sent him to your darling mother, soon he will return.'
Onwards he spurs his black horse, makes for his mother's home,
'Mother, where is my Constantine? Mother, where is my son?'
'It's two days since I saw him last, three days since I kissed him,
and if I don't see him by nightfall I'm sure to lose my wits.'
Onwards he spurs his black horse, makes for home again.
'Bitch, where is my Constantine, my little Constantinos?'
'He must have found a game to play; he'll be somewhere playing.'
'Woman, give me a bite to eat, make my midday meal,
so I can leap the mountain peaks, so I can leap the cliffs,
so I will find my Constantine, the seedling of my heart.'

And so she served the liver to him on a silver platter.
And with the first bite that he took,
the liver began to babble:
'If you're a dog, gobble me up, a stranger throw me out,
and if you are my father, bend down to me and kiss me.'
He spat his mouthful out at once, cast his eyes around him,
his heart was choked and welling up, the light in him was darkened,
tears came flowing like a stream, he almost toppled over.
But then again he steeled himself, drew his Damascus sword,
and thrust it at the woman's neck, lopped her head right off.
He cut it up in little bits, laid them in the sun,
and from the sun into a bag, from the bag out to the mill.

Κι ο μύλος εξεράλεθε κι η φτερωτή ετραγούδα.
«Άλεθε, μύλο μου, άλεθε κακής κούρβας κεφάλι,
κάνε τ' αλεύρια κόκκινα και την πασπάλη μαύρη,
για να 'ρχουνται οι γραμματικοί να παίρνουν για μελάνι,
για να 'ρχουνται κι οι όμορφες να παίρνουν κοκκινάδι».

And while the mill was grinding round, its blade began to sing:
'Grind, O mill, and grind again, grind this bitch's head,
and make the flour red as blood, make the powder black:
the clerks will take the black and use it for their ink,
the pretty girls will take the red and use it for their rouge.'

Ο πραματευτής

Πραματευτής κατέβαινε 'πό μέσ' απ' τα μπαλκάνια·
σέρνει μουλάρια δώδεκα ασήμι φορτωμένα.
Στη στράτα όπου πάγαινε, στη στράτα που παγαίνει,
αχ τραγουδούσε κι έλεγε, αχ τραγουδά και λέει:

«Καλότυχα τούτ' τα βουνά και τούτα τα μπαλκάνια,
κλέβδες όπου δεν έχουνε, κλέβδες που δε λαλάνε».
Το λόγο δεν απόσωσε, τη συντυχιά δεν είπε,
αυτού και κλέβδες έφτακαν, αυτού και κλέβδες ήρταν.
Ένας τον κόφτει τα σκοινιά, γι-άλλος τα ξεφορτώνει.
Πραματευτής παρακαλά και φρόνιμα τους λέει:

«Χαρίστ', αδέρφια μ', τ' άλογα, χαρίστε τα μουλάρια,
τ' ασήμ' αφήστε, αδέρφια μου, χαρίστε με τ' ασήμι.
Τα χέρια μου ραϊστηκαν ώς δω για να τα φέρω».

Πρωτόκλεφτος σαν τ' άκουσε πολύ τού βαροφάγκε.
Το μαχαιράκι τ' έβγαλε και στην καρδιά τ' το βάλλει.
Γαίμα το στόμα τ' γέμισε, καρδίτσα του φαρμάκι,
κι η γλώσσα τ' αηδονάλαλη λόγια πικρά αρχίν'σε·
«Πού είσαι, μάνα μ', να με δεις, κύρη μ', να με γλιτώσεις».

Πρωτόκλεφτος σαν τ' άκουσε απ' την καρδιά τ' λυπήθ'κε
και κάθισε κι αρχίνισε να τον βαριοξετάζει.

«Πούθ' είναι σένα η μάνα σου, πούθ' είναι κι ο μπαμπάς σου;»

The Merchant

There was a merchant passing through the mountains of the Balkans,
leading twelve mules in his train, all laden with silver.
And as he went along his path, as he went his way,
O he was singing and he was speaking, and as he sings he says,

'How blessed these mountains are, how blessed are all the Balkans,
there are no brigands in these parts, no brigands to trouble us.'
He hadn't even finished his words
when the brigands came upon him.
One cut the ropes, another took his silver.
And so the merchant pleads with them, speaks to them so shrewdly,

'Brothers, give me back my mules, give me back my horses.
Brothers, leave off my silverware, give me back my silver.
My hands have been crippled just to bring it here.'

The brigand chief heard his words, they sickened him inside.
He took his dagger from his belt and pierced the merchant's heart.
His mouth filled and choked with blood, his heart filled with poison,
and his once nightingale-sweet voice spoke words turned bitter,
'Mother, where are you now for me? Father, won't you save me?'

The brigand chief, soon as he heard, was saddened in his heart,
and drew up at the merchant's side and made his inquisition,

'Merchant, where is your mother from? And what about your father?'

«Η μάνα μ' 'πό τα Γιάννινα, μπαμπάς μ' από την Προύσα».
«Πόσα αδέρφια ήσασταν, σαν πόσα αδερφάκια;»
«Τρία αδέρφια ήμασταν τα τρία 'πό μια μάνα.
'Γώ είμαι ο πραματευτής κι ο γι-άλλος στο ζευγάρι,
κι ο τρίτος ο μικρότερος δώδεκα χρόνια κλέφτης».

Σαν τ' άκουσε πρωτόκλεφτος πολύ τού βαροφάγκε
κι από το χέρ' τον άδραξε και στ' άλογο τον ρίχνει
και στο γιατρό τον πάγαινε και στο γιατρό τον πάει.

«Εσύ, γιατρέ μ', καλέ γιατρέ μ', γιατρεύ'ς τον κόσμο όλο,
και τούτον γιάτρεψε το νιο τον καρδιοχτυπημένο».
«Πολλούς γιαράδες γιάτρεψα κι άλλους θενά γιατρέψω,
μ' αυτό 'ναι 'δερφοβάριμα και γιατρεμό δεν έχει».

'My mother is from Yannena, my father is from Bursa.'
'How many brothers were you all? What siblings did you have?'
'O we were brothers, brothers three, all three from the same mother.
I, the eldest, became a merchant, the second drives the oxen,
and the third, the youngest, for twelve years is a brigand.'

The brigand chief heard his words, they sickened him inside,
he swept the merchant up and threw him on his horse;
he set him on his horse, took him to the physician.

'O good physician of mine, you cure so many people.
So cure this young man too, with a death wound on his heart.'
'Many wounds have I cured, and I will cure yet others,
but there's no cure in this wide world for a wound dealt by a brother.'

Το γεφύρι της Άρτας

Σαρανταπέντε μάστοροι κι εξήντα μαθητάδες
γεφύρι θεμελιώνανε στης Άρτας το ποτάμι.
Ολημερίς εχτίζανε, το βράδυ γκρεμιζόταν.
Μοιριολογούνε μάστοροι και κλαίνε μαθητάδες:

«Αλίμονο στούς κόπους μας, κρίμα στη δούλεψή μας,
ολημερίς να χτίζομε, το βράδυ να γκρεμιέται».

Και το στοιχειό 'ποκρίθηκε απ' τη δεξιά καμάρα:

«Α δε στοιχειώσετ' άνθρωπο, τοίχος δε θεμελιώνει.
Και μη στοιχειώστε ορφανό, μη ξένο, μη διαβάτη,
παρά του πρωτομάστορα την όμορφη γυναίκα».

Τ' ακούει ο πρωτομάστορας, ραγίζει η καρδιά του.
Με το πουλί παρήγγειλε, με το πουλί τ' αηδόνι:
«Αργά ντυθεί, αργά 'λλαχτεί, αργά να πα' το γιόμα,
αργά να πά' και να διαβεί της Άρτας το γεφύρι».

Και το πουλι παράκουσε κι αλλιώς επήγε κι είπε:
«Γοργά ντυθείς, γοργά 'λλαχτείς, γοργά να πας το γιόμα,
γοργά να πας και να διαβείς της Άρτας το γεφύρι».

Νά την και εξεφάνηκε από την άσπρη στράτα.
Την είδ' ο πρωτομάστορας, ραγίζεται η καρδιά του.

The Bridge of Arta

There were forty-five stonemasons, and sixty apprentices
and they were all building a bridge across the river at Arta.
All day long they built it up, at night it tumbled down.
The stonemasons sang a lament, the apprentices were weeping.

'A shame for all our wasted toil, a pity for our labour,
all day long we build it up, at night it tumbles down!'

And then the spirit answered them from the bridge's right-hand arch,

'If you don't give a human spirit, the stones will not hold fast.
And do not give some orphan soul, a wayfarer, a stranger,
but only give the lovely wife of the master builder.'

The master builder heard these words; his heart shivered inside him.
He sent a message with a bird, with a nightingale,
'Slowly dress and slowly change, slowly bring the meal,
and then be slow to go across, to cross the bridge of Arta.'

The little bird misheard the words—it spoke them otherwise,
'Swiftly dress and swiftly change, swiftly bring the meal,
and then be swift to go across, to cross the bridge of Arta.'

Now here she is! She has appeared on the dusty way.
The master builder saw her there; his heart shivered inside him.

«Ώρα καλή σας, μάστορες κι εσείς οι μαθητάδες·
μα τι έχει ο πρωτομάστορας κι είν’ έτσι χολιασμένος;»
«Το δαχτυλίδι τού ’πεσε στην πρώτη την καμάρα,
και ποιος να μπει, και ποιος να βγει, το δαχτυλίδι νά ’βρει;»
«Εγώ να μπω, εγώ να βγω, το δαχτυλίδι νά ’βρω».

Μηδέ καλά κατέβηκε, μηδέ στη μέση μπήκε:
«Τράβα, καλέ, την άλυσο, τράβα την αλυσίδα,
όλο τον κόσμο γύρισα και τίποτα δεν ηύρα».

Ένας πιχάει με το μυστρί κι άλλος με τον ασβέστη,
πιάνει κι ο πρωτομάστορας και ρίχτει μέγα λίθο.

«Τρεις αδερφάδες ήμαστε κι οι τρεις κακογραμμένες,
η μιά ’χτισε το Δούναβη, κι η άλλη τον Αφράτη,
κι εγώ η πιο μικρότερη της Άρτας το γεφύρι.
Ως τρέμει η καρδούλα μου, ας τρέμει το γεφύρι·
ως πέφτουν τα μαλλάκια μου, να πέφτουν οι διαβάτες».

«Κόρη, τον λόγο άλλαξε κι άλλη κατάρα δώσε,
κι έεις αδερφό στην ξενιτιά, μη λάχει και περάσει».
«Σίδερο η καρδούλα μου, σίδερο το γεφύρι·
σίδερο τα μαλλάκια μου, σίδερο κι οι διαβάτες».

'Good day to you, stonemasons; good day, apprentices.
But tell me, what is with your master—why is he bile green?'
'His ring has dropped from off his finger into the bridge's arch,
and who'll go in and who'll come out and who will find the ring?'
'I will go in, I will come out and I will find the ring.'

She'd hardly gone down into it, she hadn't reached her waist,
'Pull up,' she said, 'pull up the chain, heave up those iron bindings,
I've looked around the entire place and haven't found a thing.'

One man shovels with the trowel, another adds the lime,
and the master takes a giant stone and places it on top.

'O we were sisters, sisters three, all three of us ill-fated.
The eldest built the Danube bridge, the second the Euphrates,
and I, the youngest of them all, I built the bridge of Arta.
And as my heart trembles inside, may the bridge tremble too,
and as my strands of hair fall out, may the wayfarers fall too.'

'Young woman, change your words and cast another curse,
for you too have a brother abroad, and he could chance to pass.'
'So make my heart of iron, then, make the bridge of iron;
and make my strands of hair of iron, iron the wayfarers.'

Ο Χάρος και ο νιος

Τρώτε και πίνετ' άρχοντες, κι εγώ να σας δηγούμαι.
Κι εγώ να σάς εδηγηθώ για έναν αντρωμένο,
για ένα νιόν τον είδα 'γώ στσι κάμπους και κυνήγα,
κυνήγα και λαγώνευγεν ο νιος κι αγριμολόγα.
Στο γλάκιο πιάνει ο νιος λαγό, στον πήδο πιάν' αγρίμι,
την πέρδικα την πλουμιστή οπίσω την αφήνει.
Μα ο Χάροντας επέρασε κι ήτονε μανισμένος.

«Έβγαλε, νιε, τα ρούχα σου, βγάλε και τ' άρματά σου,
δέσε τα χέρια σου σταυρό, να πάρω την ψυχή σου».
«Δε βγάνω 'γώ τα ρούχα μου, μηδέ και τ' άρματά μου,
μηδέ τα χέρια μου σταυρό, να πάρεις την ψυχή μου.
Μ' άντρας εσύ, άντρας κι εγώ, κι οι δυό καλ' αντρωμένοι,
κι άιντε να πά' παλέψομε στο σιδερόν αλώνι,
να μη ραΐσουν τα βουνά και να χαλάσει η χώρα».

Επήγαν κι απαλέψανε στο σιδερόν αλώνι,
κι εννιά φορές τον έβαλεν ο νιος το Χάρο κάτω
κι απάνω εις τς εννιά φορές του Χάρου κακοφάνη.
Πιάνει το νιό 'πού τα μαλλιά, χάμαις τον γονατίζει.

«Άφησ' με, Χάρο, απ' τα μαλλιά και πιάσ' μ' απού τα μπράτσα,
και τοτεσάς σού δείχνω γω πώς είν' τα παλικάρια».
«Από κειδά τα πιάνω γω ούλαν τα παλικάρια,
πιάνω κοπέλες όμορφες κι άντρες πολεμιστάδες,
και πιάνω και μωρά παιδιά μαζί με τσι μανάδες».

Charos and the Young Man

Eat and drink, noblemen, and I will tell a tale.
And I will tell a tale of a brave young man,
a young man that I saw myself out hunting in the plains,
hunting and stalking, chasing hares and beasts of every kind.
On the run he caught the hares, with a leap the beasts,
and the spangled partridges he left them in his stride.
But then it was that Charos passed, hot-headed, in a fury.

'Take off your clothes, young man, remove your weapons;
cross your hands and bind the wrists, so I can take your soul.'
'Charos, I won't take off my clothes, I won't remove my weapons,
Charos, I won't bind my wrists for you to take my soul.
But you're a man and I'm a man and both of us are brave,
so come, let's fight it out upon the iron-hard threshing floor,
let's see then if the mountains crack and if the country's ruined.'

And so they went and wrestled on the iron-hard threshing floor,
and nine times did the young man throw Charos to the ground,
and on the ninth time he was thrown, Charos was enraged.
He grabbed the young man by the hair, and brought him to his knees.

'Let go, Charos, leave off my hair, wrestle me by my arms,
and then I'll fairly show you what fine young men are made of.'
'It's by the hair I grab them all, all the fine young men;
the lovely girls, I grab them too, warriors and others;
I grab the little children too, the babes with their mothers.'

Το Πάλεμα του Τσαμαδού και του γιου του

Μέσ' στ' αϊ-Γιωργιού τους πλάτανους γένονταν πανηγύρι,
το πανηγύρι ήταν πολύ, κι ο τόπος ήταν λίγος,
δώδεκα δίπλες ο χορός, κι εξηνταδυό τραπέζια,
και χίλια ψένονται σφαχτά σ' όλο το πανηγύρι.
Κι οι γέροντες παρακαλούν, τάζουν στον αϊ-Γιώργη,
ο Τσαμαδός να μην ερθεί, χαλάει το πανηγύρι.

Ακόμα ο λόγος έστεκε κι ο Τσαμαδός εφάνη,
που ροβολάει οχ το βουνό κατά το πανηγύρι.
Πατεί και σειέται το βουνό, κράζει κι αχάν οι λόγγοι,
κι εκράταγε στον ώμο του δέντρο ξεριζωμένο,
και απάνου στα κλωνάρια του θεριά είχε κρεμασμένα.
«Ώρα καλή σας, γέροντες» – «Καλώς το παλικάρι».
«Ποιος έχει αστήθι μάρμαρο και χέρια σιδερένια,
για νά 'βγει να παλέψουμε στο μαρμαρένιο αλώνι;»
Κανείς δεν αποκρίθηκε απ' τους πανηγυριώτες
της χήρας γιος εφώναξε, της χήρας ο αντρειωμένος:
«Εγώ 'χω αστήθι μάρμαρο και χέρια σιδερένια,
για νά 'βγω να παλέψουμε στο μαρμαρένιο αλώνι».

Βγαίνουν κι οι δυο με τα σπαθιά και πάνε να παλέψουν.
Εκεί που επάτειε ο Τσαμαδός εβούλιαζε τ' αλώνι,
κι εκεί που επάτειε το παιδί εβούλιαζε κ' εβύθα.
Εκεί που βάρειε ο Τσαμαδός το γαίμα πάει ποτάμι,
κι εκεί που χτύπαε το παιδί τα κόκαλα τσακίζει.
«Κοντοκαρτέρει, βρε παιδί, κάτι να σε ρωτήσω.

The Struggle between Tsamados and His Son

Among the plane trees of St George there was a festival:
the festival was large; St George's spot was small,
the dance spiralled twelve times round, among sixty-two tables;
a thousand heads were killed for all the festival.
The elders pleaded with St George, vowed him offerings,
that Tsamados be kept away—he wrecks the festival.

The words were still upon the air when Tsamados appeared,
tearing down the mountainside towards the festival.
When he steps the mountain shakes, he cries and the valleys ring;
and on his shoulder he bore down the trunk of an uprooted tree,
and on its branches he had hung the corpses of wild beasts.
'Greetings, elders, and good day'—'Good day to you, fine fellow'.
'Who here has a marble chest and hands of iron,
and will come out and fight with me on the marble threshing floor?'
No one responded to Tsamados, not one of the revellers,
until the widow's son cried out, the brave son of the widow:
'It's I that have a marble chest and hands of iron,
I will come out and fight with you on the marble threshing floor.'

The two went out with swords in hand, they went to fight each other.
When Tsamados trod on the ground, the threshing floor sunk down,
and when the young man trod the ground, it sunk and foundered.
When Tsamados struck the boy, his blood ran like a river,
and when the boy struck Tsamados, he made his bones shatter.
'Hold on, young man, not so fast—let me ask you something.

Ποια σκύλα μάνα σ' έκαμε, κι ο κύρης σου ποιος ήταν;»
«Η μάνα μου όταν χήρεψε δεν μ' είχε γεννημένον,
κι όμοιασα του πατέρα μου και θα τον απεράσω».
Από το χέρι τον αρπά στης μάνας του να πάνε.
Από μακριά τούς ε-θωρεί κι ετοίμασε τραπέζι.
Κι εκεί που τρώγαν κι έπιναν η χήρα τούς κερνούσε,
κρασί κερνάει τον Τσαμαδό, φαρμάκι το παιδί της.
«Μανούλα, μ' εφαρμάκωσες, απ' το θεό να τό 'βρεις!»

What bitch was it that mothered you, what man was your father?'
'My mother, when she was widowed, she hadn't given birth to me,
and I was like my father, and I will overcome him.'
Tsamados grabbed the boy's hand, they went to find his mother.
She saw them from afar and she prepared a table.
And as they drank and as they ate, she poured them each a drink,
wine she poured for Tsamados, poison for her son.
'Mother, you have poisoned me; you'll answer unto God!'

Tsamados is a character of uncertain origin, but he bears some resemblance to
Charos. In some versions of this song, the son does not die: in one case, he per-
ceives his mother's treachery before drinking from the cup; in another, he
inherits his father's kingdom.

SONGS OF GREEKS FAR FROM HOME

The necessarily long-winded English translation of this title conceals just one word in Greek, *xeniteia*, a concept that was (and is) known throughout the Greek world. *Xeniteia* is the opposite of *patrida* (homeland) and denotes the condition of being abroad—or more specifically, being away from the village of one's birth—for long periods of time, perhaps for a whole lifetime.

While Greeks have a long history of going abroad, most of the songs here refer to the mass emigration from the Greek mainland that began in the seventeenth century, when the villages could not support their growing populations. Many Greeks established enterprises throughout the Balkans, particularly in what is now Romania—in 'Vlachia' (Wallachia), 'Bogdania' (Moldova) and 'Black Bucharest'— as well as in the Middle East. It was customary for young men to leave their village as soon as they were married, to return only years later for a brief stay to father another child before promptly leaving again.

It was the women left at home who composed these songs, in which fathers are glaringly absent. The women's words voice the sense of injustice and loss suffered by the village as a whole from the absence of their menfolk. Many of the songs draw on themes, images and phraseology from the ritual laments, while being poignantly aware that this painful tradition of absence, unsanctified by formal ritual, had 'no consolation'.

Τώρα 'ναι Μάης κι άνοιξη

Τώρα 'ναι Μάης κι άνοιξη, τώρα 'ναι καλοκαίρι
τώρα κι η γης στολίζεται εννιά λοϊών λουλούδια
με πράσινα, με κόκκινα και στην κορφή με φύλλα·
τώρα κι ο ξένος βούλεται να πάνει στα δικά του.
Νύχτα σελώνει τ' άλογο, νύχτα το καλιγώνει
φκιάν' ασημένια πέταλα, καρφιά μαλαματένια,
κι η κόρη οπού τον αγαπάει, κι η κόρη οπού τον έχει,
παίρνει κηρί και τό 'φεγγε, ποτήρ' και τον κερνάει·
«Πάρε μ', αφέντη μ', πάρε με, πάρε κι εμέ κοντά σου
να φκιάνω δείπνο να δειπνάς, γιόμα να γιοματίζεις
να σ' στρώνω πέντε στρώματα, πέντε προσκεφαλάκια».
«Πού να σε πάρω, κόρη μου, πού να σε σκαπετίσω;
Εκεί κορίτσια δεν περνούν, γυναίκες δεν διαβαίνουν,
εσένα παίρνουν, κόρη μου, και μένα με σκοτώνουν».

Now it's May and Now It's Spring

Now it's May and now it's spring, now it is the summer,
now is the earth adorned with nine kinds of flowers,
with the green and with the red, the topmost tree in leaf.
It's now the stranger wants to leave, to go unto his own.
By dark of night he saddles his horse, by dark of night he shoes it,
he makes its shoes of silver, the nails he makes of gold,
and there's a girl who loves him, there's a girl who has him,
she takes a candle, brings him light, pours him a cup to drink.
'Take me with you, master, take me along beside you,
I'll make you dinner every day, I'll make the midday meal,
I'll lay five mattresses for your bed, five pillows for your head.'
'How can I take you, lovely one, and spirit you away?
Where I'm going, girls don't go, women don't travel there—
they'll take you away, lovely one, and they'll murder me.'

The man who goes abroad is himself described as a 'stranger' (*xenos*), as if the strangeness of foreign lands has been indelibly stuck to him. This is a usage also common to the songs of marriage and the ritual laments.

Η συζυγική εγκατάλειψις

Μάνα μ', γιατί με πάντρεψες και μό 'δωκες βλαχιώτη;
Δώδεκα χρόνους στη Βλαχιά και τρεις βραδιές στο σπίτι.
Τρίτη βραδιά, πικρή βραδιά, δυο ώρες πριν να φέξει,
άπλωσα το χεράκι μου, τον άντρα μου δε βρίσκω·
εις το κατώϊ αρρέντεψα, δε βρίσκω τ' άλογό του
γυρίζω, τρέχω στον οντά, δε βρίσκω τ' άρματά του
και στο κρεβάτ' ακούμπησα να πω το μοιρολόγι:
«Μωρ' έρημο προσκέφαλο, μωρ' έρημό μου στρώμα,
το πού 'ν' αφέντης πού 'χεταν απόψε πλαγιασμένο;»
«Αφέντης μας μάς άφηκε και πάει στο ταξίδι
μέσα στην έρημη Βλαχιά, στο μαύρο Μπουκουρέστι».

The Wife of the Man Abroad

Mother, why did you marry me off and give me to that Wallachian?
He's twelve years in Wallachia and just three nights at home.
And on the third, the bitter night, two hours before the dawn,
I stretched out and reached for him; my husband wasn't there.
I hastened to the basement; there was no sign of his horse.
I came back running to our room; there was no sign of his weapons.
I lay back down upon the bed and began this lament,
'O wretched pillow, wretched bed, O sorry, wretched mattress,
where's the master who was tonight lying here beside me?'
'Our master has abandoned us and gone out on his journey,
into wretched Wallachia, to black Bucharest.'

As in the previous song, the husband is a Wallachian by virtue of the fact that
he has gone to live in Wallachia (Vlachia in Greek). It should be noted that in
these songs Wallachia, while being a real place, is practically synonymous with
the abstract concept of *xeniteia*.

Αλησμονώ και χαίρουμαι

Αλησμονώ και χαίρουμαι, θυμιούμαι και λυπιούμαι,
θυμήθηκα την ξενιτιά και θέλω να πηγαίνω.
«Σήκω, μανά μ', και ζύμωσε καθάριο παξιμάδι».
Με πόνους βάνει το θερμό, με δάκρυα το κουφίζει
και με τ' αναστενάγματα το φούρνο συνδαυλίζει.
«Άργησε, φούρνε, να καείς και συ, ψωμί, να γένεις
για να περάσει ο κερατζής να μείνει ο γιος μου πίσω».

Forgetfulness Brings Happiness

Forgetfulness brings happiness, memory brings sadness—
now I've remembered being abroad, and I must be going.
'Mother, get up and knead the dough; Mother, bake me the rusks.'
She waters it with suffering, she kneads it with her tears,
and with the pining of her heart she fires up the oven.
'Oven, be slow in heating up; bread, be slow in baking,
so that the caravan will pass, my son will not be taken.'

The young men going into the Balkans from mainland Greece were taken by caravans of mules that traditionally left the villages on 14 September (the Feast of the Exaltation of the Holy Cross), arriving in Bucharest one month later. The drivers of these caravans often achieved semi-mythical status, partly because of the wealth they accrued, partly because of their pied-piper-like activities in spiriting away the young men.

Η ξενιτιά είν' βαρύτερη

Η φυλακή κι η ξενιτιά, ν-η φτώχεια κι η αρφάνια,
τα τέσσερα ζυγιάστηκαν μ' ένα χρυσό στατέρι,
να ιδούν ποιο είν' βαρύτερο, βαρύτερ' από τ' άλλα·
η ξενιτιά είν' βαρύτερη, βαρύτερη από τ' άλλα.

To Be Far From Home

Being in jail or far from home, being poor or an orphan,
were all weighed up, the four of them, on a golden balance,
to see which weighed the heaviest, heavier than the others;
being far from home weighed heaviest, heavier than the others.

Ο ζωντανός ξεχωρισμός

Παρηγοριά έχ' ο θάνατος και λησμονιά ο Χάρος
μα ο ζωντανός ξεχωρισμός παρηγοριά δεν έχει.
Χωρίζ' η μάνα το παιδί και το παιδί τη μάνα,
χωρίζονται τ' αντρόγυνα τα πολυαγαπημένα,
και κει που ξεχωρίζονται χορτάρι δε φυτρώνει.

The Living Separation

Death has its consolation, yes, and Charos oblivion,
but for the living separation there is no consolation.
The mother is parted from her child, the child from the mother,
beloved husband, beloved wife are parted from each other,
and in the place they separate, grass won't sprout again.

Ξενιτεμένο μου πουλί

Ξινιτιμένου μου πουλί κί παραπουνιμένου,
η ξινιτιά σι χαίριτι κι 'γώ 'χου τουν καημό σου.
Τι να σου στείλου, ξένι μου, τι να σου προυβουδήσου;
Να στείλου μήλου σέπιτι, κυδώνι μαραγκιάζει
να στείλου μουσκουστάφυλου κι αυτό μού σταφιδιάζει·
να στείλου κί του δάκρυ μου σ' ένα χρυσό μαντίλι,
του δάκρυ μ' είνι καφτιρό κί καίει του μαντίλι.

Bird of Mine That's Far Abroad

Bird of mine that's far abroad, bird of mine that's pining,
strange lands now have joy of you, while I am deep in sorrow.
What can I send you over there; what can I send you, stranger?
I send an apple and it rots, a quince and it withers,
I send a sweet-perfumed grape, it wrinkles to a raisin.
So in a golden kerchief I send a tear to you,
my tear is hot, so hot it burns the kerchief.

The last five lines of this song are common also to ritual laments, where the
mourner imagines sending the same items to the lost loved one in the underworld.

Γιάννη μου, το μαντίλι σου

Γιάννη μου, το μαντίλι σου τι τό 'χεις λερωμένο;
«Το λέρωσε η ξενιτιά, τα έρημα τα ξένα,
πέντε ποτάμια τό 'πλυναν, λερώσανε κι εκείνα,
περάσαν χίλια πρόβατα και λέρωσαν κι εκείνα».

Yanni's Handkerchief

O Yanni, why's your handkerchief so very soiled and dirty?
'It's being abroad that's soiled it, those wretched foreign lands.
I've washed it in five rivers, and they too became soiled,
a thousand sheep went through the stream, and they too became
 soiled.'

Η μάγισσα

Κινήσαν τα καράβια τα Ζαγορινά,
κίνησε κι ο καλός μου, πήε στην ξενιτειά.
Δώδεκα χρόνους κάνει δίχως 'πολογιά·
μού στέλλ' ένα μαντίλι μ' είκοσι φλωριά,
και στο μαντίλι μέσα μόχει 'πολογιά.
«Θες, κόρη μου, παντρέψου, θες, καλόγρεψε.
Τι εδώ που 'μ' ο καημένος, επαντρεύτηκα·
επήρα μια γυναίκα σκύλα μάγισσα,
μαγεύει τα καράβια, δεν κινούν γι' αυτού,
μ' εμάγεψε κ' εμένα, δεν κινώ κι εγώ.
Όντας κινώ για νά 'ρθω, χιόνια και βροχές,
όντας γυρίζω πίσω, ήλιος, ξαστεριά.
Ζώνομαι τ' άρματά μου, πέφτουν καταγής,
πιάνω γραφή να γράψω, και ξεγράφεται».

The Witch

The boats set out to travel, the boats of Zagora,
my good man set out with them, he went far from home.
All twelve years that he spent there, he didn't send a word.
and then he sends a kerchief, in its folds I find
twenty silver florins, and a word from him.
'Marry if you want to—or become a nun,
but in these wretched places, I'm a married man.
The woman that I've taken is a crafty witch,
who bewitches all the boats, so they do not set out,
and she's bewitched me also, and nor do I set out.
When I set out to travel, there's only snow and rain,
when I turn back again, there's sun and cloudless skies.
When I put on my armour, it falls down to the ground,
when I begin to write, the writing comes unwritten.'

This song, which employs the rarer twelve-syllable iambic metre, refers to the village of Zagora on Mount Pelion. In the early eighteenth century, this village developed a fleet of sailing boats for trade around the Aegean and the Black Sea.

Διώχνεις με, μάνα

Διώχνεις με, μάνα, διώχνεις με, μα 'γώ να φύγω θέλω,
να 'ρθεί καιρός τ' αϊ-Γεωργιού να πας στον αϊ-Γεώργη,
να δεις τον τόπο μ' αδειανό και το στασίδι μ' έρμο,
να δεις τες νιες σαν λεμονιές, τους νιους σαν κυπαρίσσια,
να πάρεις κάτω στο γιαλό τους ναύτες να ρωτάεις.
«Ναύτες μου, ναυτοπούλια μου, μην είδετε το γιό μου;»
«Εχθέ βραδί τον είδαμε στης Μπαρμπαριάς τα μέρη,
πού 'χε τον ουρανό σκεπή, τη θάλασσα σεντόνι,
Τα χοχλιδάκια του γιαλού είχε για προσκεφάλι.
Μαύρα πουλιά τον τρώγανε, άσπρα τον τριγυρίζουν
μα ένα πουλί καλό πουλί δεν ήθελε να φάει.
"Φάε και συ, καλό πουλί, 'π' ανδρειωμένου σάρκα,
Γράψε και στη φτερούγα σου δυο λόγια πικραμένα,
να τα διαβάζει η μάνα μου να κλαί' η αδερφή μου,
να τα διαβάζει η αδερφή να κλαίει ο κόσμος όλος"».

Mother, You're Sending Me Away

Mother, you're sending me away—but it's me wants to be leaving,
and there will come St George's day, you'll go to St George's chapel,
you'll see the place left for me, you'll see my pew is empty,
you'll see the girls like lemon trees, the boys like cypresses,
and then you'll bear down to the shore, you'll go to ask the sailors:
'Sailors, darling sailors, tell me—have you seen my son?'
'Last night it was we saw him, over Barbary way,
he had the sea for his sheet, the sky his covering,
and the shells upon the shore served as his pillow.
There were black birds eating him, white ones circling round,
and there was one bird, one good bird, who wouldn't eat a morsel.
"Have your fill, good little bird, of a brave man's flesh,
but then write words upon your wings, and make them bitter,
so that my mother reads them and makes my sister weep,
so that my sister reads them too and makes the whole world weep."'

Ο θάνατος στην ξενιτιά

Παρακαλώ σε, μοίρα μου, να μη με ξενιτέψεις,
κι αν λάχει και ξενιτευτώ, θάνατο μη μου δώσεις,
εμέ είδανε τα μάτια μου τους ξένους πώς τους θάφτουν·
μηδέ λιβάνι ηδέ κερί μηδέ παπά ηδέ ψάλτη,
αλάργα από την εκκλησιά, σε χέρισο χωράφι.
Ήρθε καιρός ν' αλατρευτεί το χέρισο χωράφι.
Φέρνουν ζευγάρι απ' τα βουνά κι αλάτρι από τους κάμπους,
φέρνουν γυνί από μάστορα, καινούριο από καμίνι,
κι ο νιος οπού τα κέντουνε πολλά ήτο τεχνεμένος,
με το κοντάρι τα βαρεί, με το σπαθί τα γέρνει,
και με τ' ασημομάχαιρο αρχάει και τα κεντάει.
Πρώτη αλατριά ν-οπ' έδωκε, δεύτερη βγάνει νιόνε.
Αφήνει ο νιος τ' αλάτρεμα, και αρχάει το μοιρολόγι.
«Μα νά 'χα τέτοιον αδερφό, νά 'χα τέτοιο λεβέντη,
στη γη και δεν τον έβανα να τονε φάει το χώμα.
Ήθελα πάω σε γιαλό, κάτω σε περιγιάλι,
να κόψω κιτροκάλαμο να κάμω ωριό κιβούρι,
να βάλω πάτους βάλσαμο και πάτους καρυοφύλλι,
στη μέση τον αμάραντο να μην τονε μαράνει.

Death Abroad

O fate, one thing I ask of you—don't send me far from home,
but if it happens I go abroad, do not bring me death,
for I have seen with my own eyes how they bury strangers—
without a candle, without incense, without a priest or cantor,
far removed from the church, in some fallow field.
The time came for that fallow field, the time it would be ploughed.
A plough is carried from the plains, two oxen from the mountains,
a ploughshare from a craftsman's hand, gleaming from the furnace.
And there's a young man to goad the beasts, a man of noted skill,
with the shaft he spurs them on, with the sword he drives them,
and with the silver dagger he sets about to goad them.
On the second turn of the plough, a youthful head appears.
The young man stops his ploughing, instead starts a lament:
'Oh that I had brother like that—such a fine young man—
I'd never put him in the ground and let the soil consume him.
But I would take him to the shore, I'd take him to the sea,
and cut a yellow reed for him and make a lovely coffin,
make a bed of fragrant herbs, layers of carnations,
and place the everlasting flower, so he would never wither.'

SONGS OF LOVE AND DESIRE

The songs in this section (called *erotika* in Greek) do not make up a cohesive whole, since they do not belong to a specific ritual or to a particular group of people. They range from dance songs (*choreftika*), such as 'How Love Is Caught' (which could be performed at a wedding celebration), to improvised rhyming couplets, to table songs, deriving from ballads. This motley collection, therefore, exhibits more differences in form than the other songs, such as the unusual thirteen-syllable metre of 'The Nun' and the presence of rhyme in several songs.

Though there is no personification of love or desire, as there is of death (Charos) in the ritual laments, the songs demonstrate the metaphysical power of love in ways that are as strikingly physical as the other songs in the canon. One of the best examples—'I Kissed Red Lips'— was held by the poet George Seferis to be one of the masterpieces of the folk song tradition.

Πώς πιάνετ' η αγάπη

Εμπάτ' αγόρια στο χορό και πιάστε το τραγούδι,
πέστε και τραγουδήσετε πώς πιάνετ' η αγάπη:
«Από τα μάτια πιάνεται, στα χείλια ξεφυτρώνει,
κι από τα χείλια χύνεται και στην καρδιά ριζώνει».

How Love Is Caught

Come out, O boys, into the dance, come and take up the song,
tell, O tell and sing, O sing how love is caught;
'It's from the eyes it's caught, and in the lips it sprouts,
and from the lips comes pouring down and in the heart takes root.'

Η αγαπώ

Ή δώστε μου την αγαπώ, ή δώστε μου την θέλω
ή κάμετέ μου μαγικά, να την αλησμονήσω.
Φορήσετέ με σίδερα και ζώσετέ με βάτο,
να με βαρούν τα σίδερα, να με σκεπάζει ο βάτος,
και βάλετε εις τον κόλπον μου τρικέφαλον οφίδι,
να με δακάνει το θηριόν, να την αλησμονήσω.

The One I Love

So give to me the one I love, or give me my desire,
or do those magic spells on me, so that I forget her.
Dress me in clothes of iron, put brambles around my waist,
so that the iron crushes me, the brambles wrap around me,
then bring to me a three-headed asp and place it on my chest,
so that the beast will bite me, so that I forget her.

This song is the first published Greek folk song, appearing in the work
Turcograecia by the German humanist Martin Crusius, published in 1584.
The song was given to him by his student, Catharinus Dulcis, who travelled
to Greece and Turkey in 1565–6. He may have collected the song in Cyprus.
The version above was reconstructed into modern Greek by Manoussos
Manoussakas in 1975.

Του Δήμου

Αυτά τα μάτια
       —Δήμο μ'—
              τά 'μορφα, τα φρύδια τα γραμμένα,
       —γεια σ' αγάπη μου—
αυτά με κάμνουν
       —Δήμο μ'—
              κι αρρωστώ, με κάμνουν κι αποθαίνω.
       —γεια σ' αγάπη μου—
Γιά βγάλε
       —Δήμο μ'—
              το σπαθάκι σου, και κόψε το λαιμό μου,
       —γεια σ' αγάπη μου—
και μάσε
       —Δήμο μ'—
              και το αίμα μου σ' ένα χρυσό μανδίλι,
       —γεια σ' αγάπη μου—
και σύρ' το
       —Δήμο μ'—
              στα εννιά χωριά, στα δέκα βιλαέτια,
       —γεια σ' αγάπη μου—
κι αν σ' ερωτήσουν
       —Δήμο μ'—
              τ' είν' αυτό· το αίμα της αγάπης
       —γεια σ' αγάπη μου.

For Dimos

Those eyes of yours,
　—O Dimos—
　　　those lovely eyes, the fine-drawn lines of eyebrows,
　—O my love—
it's them that make me
　—O Dimos—
　　　ail and sicken, it's them that make me die.
　—O my love—
So go on, then,
　—O Dimos—
　　　draw your sword, draw it and cut my throat,
　—O my love—
and gather up
　—O Dimos—
　　　all of my blood, into a golden kerchief,
　—O my love—
and draw it
　—O Dimos—
　　　through nine villages, through ten vilayets,
　—O my love—
and if they ask you
　—O Dimos—
　　　what it is; say, 'the blood of love'.
　—O my love.

The interjections 'O Dimos' and 'O my love' are aspects of the performance of the song, called *tsakismata* ('cuttings'). If they are removed, the lines adhere to the same fifteen-syllable metre as the other songs.

Κόκκιν' αχείλι εφίλησα

Κόκκιν' αχείλι εφίλησα κι έβαψε το δικό μου,
και στο μαντίλι τό 'συρα κι έβαψε το μαντίλι,
και στο ποτάμι τό 'πλυνα κι έβαψε το ποτάμι,
κι έβαψε η άκρη του γιαλού κι η μέση του πελάγου.
Κατέβη ο αετός να πιει νερό κι έβαψαν τα φτερά του,
κι έβαψε ο ήλιος ο μισός και το φεγγάρι ακέριο.

I Kissed Red Lips

I kissed red lips, and those red lips dyed my lips too.
I wiped them with a kerchief, they dyed the kerchief red,
I washed the kerchief in the river, it dyed the river too;
the river dyed the shoreline edge and the middle of the sea.
An eagle came to quench its thirst, its wings were dyed red too,
and half the sun was dyed red and the circle of the moon.

Ο κλέφτης του φιλιού

Εγώ περνώ και δε μιλώ κι η κόρη χαιρετά με.
«Πού πάγεις, κλέφτη του φιλιού και κομπωτή τς αγάπης;»
«Μ' αν είμαι κλέφτης του φιλιού και κομπωτής τς αγάπης,
τι μού 'δινες τα χείλη σου κι εγλυκοφίλησά τα;»
«Κι α σού 'δωκα τα χείλη μου κι εγλυκοφίλησές τα,
νύχτα ήτο, ποιος μας ένιωσε, κι αυγή, ποιος μας εθώρει;»
«Τ' άστρο τς αυγής το λαμπερό, εκείνο μας εθώρει,
και τ' άστρο ν-εχαμήλωσε και τό 'πε του θαλάσσου,
και το θαλάσσι του κουπιού, και το κουπί του ναύτη,
κι ο ναύτης το διαλάλησε στη γη την οικουμένη».

The Thief of Kisses

I walk past and say not a word; the lovely girl greets me.
'Where are you going, you thief of kisses, you trickster of love?'
'If I am a thief of kisses, a trickster of love,
why did you let me have your lips and let me sweetly kiss them?'
'If I let you have my lips and let you sweetly kiss them,
who noticed us by dark of night? At dawn, who could have seen us?'
'The morning star that gleams so bright—it was the star that saw us,
and the morning star bent to the sea, and told it everything,
and the sea was quick to tell the oar, the oar to tell the sailor,
and now the sailor's bruited it to the whole wide universe.'

Ο Κουλοχέρης

Στογ Γαλατά στα μάρμαρα, στα μάρμαρα, στημ Πόλη,
άουρος πέτραπ πελεκά και λείπ᾽ η μιά του χέρα.
Κόρη ξανθή τονε θωρεί απού το παραθύρι.
«Πρόλαε, μάνα μου, να ᾽εις αυτό τοκ κουτσοχέρη,
που πελεκά τα μάρμαρα μόνομ με τό ᾽να χέρι».
«Κόρη, γιατί μ᾽ ανεελάς, γιατί με ανεμπαίτζεις;
Εννιά κορίτσια φίλησα και δυόεκα χηράες
και δεκαπέντε καλογριές κι εκόψαμ μου το χέρι.
Χριστέ, να φίλησα κι εσέ, κι ας μού ᾽κοβγακ και τ᾽ άλλο».

The One-Armed Man

In the marble works at Galata, the marble works in the City,
there's a young man hewing stone, and he has one arm missing.
Then from a window up above a girl looks down at him.
'Mother, come quick and have a look at this one-armed man,
who cuts the marble slab by slab, who cuts with one arm only.'
'Girl, why do you deride me so? Girl, why do you mock me?
I kissed nine lovely girls, I kissed twelve widows also,
and fifteen nuns I kissed them too, that's why they cut my arm off.
Christ, that I had kissed you too, and let them cut off the other!'

Galata is a district in Istanbul (here simply called 'the City').

Καλόγραια

Κάτω στην αγιά Μαρίνα και στην Παναγιά,
δώδεκα χρονώ κορίτσι γίν'κε καλογριά,
με σταυρό, με κομπολόγι, πάν' στην εκκλησιά,
κι ούδε το σταυρό της κάνει, κι ούδε προσκυνά.
Τα παλικαράκια βλέπει με πολύν καημό·
βγήκε μες στο σταυροδρόμι και κρασί πουλεί,
διάβηκ' ένας, διάβηκ' άλλος, διάβηκα κι εγώ.
«Καλή μέρα σου, καλόγρια, κι αμέ τι πουλείς;»
«Και κρασί πουλώ, λεβέντη, και καλό ρακί».
«Καλογριά μου, σαν μεθύσω, πού θα κοιμηθώ;»
«Παλικάρι μ', αν μεθύσεις, έλα στο κελί,
πόχω πέρδικα ψημένη και γλυκό κρασί,
πόχω πάπλωμα στρωμένο και χρυσό χαλί,
που είμαι κόρη και κοιμούμαι μόν' και μοναχή·
για να φάμε και να πιούμε και να παίξουμε,
να φιλήσεις, ν' αγκαλιάσεις καλογριάς κορμί».
«Τσώπα, τσώπα, καλογριά μου, κι είναι αντροπή».
«Αντροπή 'ναι στα κορίτσια και στις όμορφες,
και σ' εμένα την καλόγρια δεν είν' αντροπή,
που είμ' στα ράσα τυλιγμένη σα χλωρό τυρί».

The Nun

Down at Saint Marina's place, at the Virgin's spot,
there's a girl of twelve years old, given as a nun,
with her cross and chaplet she goes into the church,
but no she doesn't cross herself, she doesn't kneel to pray.
And all the handsome, fine young men look on her so glum.
So she goes out to the crossroads to sell her flasks of wine,
one went past and then another, and then I passed her too,
'Good morning to you, lovely nun; pray, what do you sell?
It's wine I'm selling, handsome man; I'm selling *raki* too.'
'But what if I get drunk, good nun; pray, where can I sleep?'
'If you get drunk, my handsome man, come into my cell,
where I have a partridge roasting, where I have sweet wine,
where I will have laid out blankets and a golden rug.
For I'm a lovely girl who's sleeping lonesome and alone;
and we will eat and we will drink and later we will play,
and you can kiss, you can embrace the body of a nun.'
'Hush, my good nun, and be silent, it's shameful what you say.'
'If it's shameful for the beauties and for all the girls,
so why is it not shameful, too, for a lovely nun like me—
to be wrapped up in my habit like a fresh cheese?'

Η παπαδοπούλα

Ένα κομμάτι σύγνεφο κι ένα κομμάτ' αντάρα!
Κι ουδέ κομμάτι σύγνεφο κι ουδέ κομμάτ' αντάρα,
μόν' είν' η κόρη του παπά πόρχετ' από τ' αμπέλι.
Βαστά τα μήλα στην ποδιά, τα ρόιδα στο μαντίλι·
άγουρο συναπάντησε και της γυρεύει μήλα.
«Πάρε τα μήλα που βαστώ, τα ρόιδα που βαστάω».
«Δε θέλω 'γώ τα μήλα σου, τα τσαλαπατημένα,
μόν' θέλω 'γώ του κόρφου σου τα μοσκομυρισμένα».

The Priest's Daughter

A piece of cloud and a piece of mist!
But that is no piece of cloud, that is no piece of mist,
it is the daughter of the priest, who's coming from the vines,
with pomegranates in her scarf and apples in her apron,
and there she meets a young man, who asks her for her apples.
'Here, take my pomegranates, the apples that I'm holding.'
'It's not those apples that I want, those trampled apples,
it's the apples of your bosom, the ones that smell so sweet.'

Της απαρνημένης

Χρυσό λαμπρό φεγγάρι μου, που πας να βασιλέψεις,
χαιρέτα μου τον αγαπώ, τον κλέφτη της αγάπης.
Αυτός μ' εφίλειε κι έλεγε: «ποτέ δε σ' απαρνιούμαι»,
και τώρα μ' απαρνήθηκε σαν καλαμιά στον κάμπο,
σαν εκκλησιά αλειτούργητη, σα χώρα κουρσεμένη.
Θέλω να τον καταραστώ και πάλε τον λυπούμαι,
και μου πονούν τα σπλάχνα μου, πονεί και η ψυχή μου.
Μα κάλλι' ας τον καταραστώ κι ας κάμ' ο Θιός τι θέλει.

«Σε κυπαρίσσι ν' ανεβεί να πάρει το λουλούδι,
από ψηλά να κρημνιστεί και χαμηλά να πέσει,
σαν το γυαλί να συντριφτεί, σαν το κερί να λιώσει,
να πέσ' εις τούρκικα σπαθιά, εις φράγκικα μαχαίρια,
πέντε γιατροί να τον κρατούν και δέκα να τον γιάνουν,
κι εγώ εκείθε να διαβώ και να τους ξαγναντέψω.

"Καλώς τα κάνετε, γιατροί, καλώς τα πολεμάτε,
ας κόβουν τα ξουράφια σας, μη σας πονεί η ψυχή σας·
γιατί παινιούνταν κι έλεγε πως δε με απαρνιέται,
και τώρα μ' απαρνήθηκε σαν καλαμιά στον κάμπο.
Ανοίξτε τ' όλες τες πληγές οπόχει στο κορμί του,
έχω πανιά για το ξαντό, σεντόνια να του στρώσω.
Κι αν δε δυνάσουν τα πανιά, κόβω και την ποδιά μου·
κι αν δε δυνάσει κι η ποδιά, κόβω και το βελέσι·
κι αν θέλει αίμα γιατρικό, πάρετ' οχ την καρδιά μου"».

The Abandoned Girl

Golden gleaming moon of mine, why are you going to set?
Go and greet that love of mine, that thief of love.
He kissed me and he said to me, 'I'll never abandon you,'
and now he has abandoned me like the stubble of the field,
like a church without a liturgy, like a country plundered.
I want to curse him again and again, and then I pity him,
and in my spleen I yearn for him, my soul is yearning too.
But it's better that I curse—let God do as He wills!

'May he climb a cypress tree to pick its crowning flower,
and may he tumble down and fall to the ground,
and may he smash like a pane of glass, may he melt like wax,
may he fall on Frankish swords, fall on Turkish sabres,
and five physicians tend to him and ten look after him—
it's then that I will wander past and look on them from far.

"Well done, physicians, you're faring well, you're battling it well,
but do not let it trouble you, to let your sharp blades cut him,
because he boasted and he said he wouldn't abandon me,
and now he has abandoned me like the stubble of the field.
So open all the wounds on him, the wounds across his body,
and I have cloths to cover them, sheets to lay beneath him.
And if the cloths do not succeed, I'll cut a piece of apron,
and if my apron does not succeed, I'll cut my petticoat,
if he needs blood for remedy, take it from my heart."'

Για ένα ζευγάρι ρόδα

Μια κόρη ρόδα εμάζευε κι ανθούς εκορφολόγα
κι ο γιος του ρήγα επέρασε περδικοκυνηγώντας.
Δυο ρόδα τής εζήτησε και τέσσερα τού δίνει
κι η μάννα τση την έβλεπε από το παρεθύρι.
«Σώπα να 'ρθούν τα 'δέρφια σου κι α δε σε μαρτυρήσω...»
Το βράδυ ήρθαν τα 'δέρφια τση κι ευθύς τη μαρτυράει.
Ο ένας την πιάνει απ' τα μαλλιά κι ο άλλος απ' το χεράκι,
κι οληνυχτίς τη δέρνανε μ' ένα χρυσό βεργάκι.
Κοντά στα ξημερώματα η κόρη εψυχομάχα.
Η μάννα τση τη ρώτησε τι ρούχα να τση βάλει.
«Μη θέλεις τα μεταξωτά, μη θες τα ρικαμάδα,
μη θες τα χρυσοπράσινα που σόχω στην κασέλα;»
«Δε θέλω τα μεταξωτά, μήτε τα ρικαμάδα,
μήτε τα χρυσοπράσινα που μόχεις στην κασέλα·
θέλω τα ρουχαλάκια μου τα καταματωμένα,
για να το μάθει η γειτονιά, για να το μάθει η χώρα,
πως μ' αδικοσκοτώσατε για 'να ζευγάρι ρόδα».

For a Pair of Roses

There was a girl out picking flowers, picking the choicest roses;
the prince, out partridge hunting, happened to pass by.
He asked two roses of the girl and she gives him four.
From a window up above her mother's looking on:
'Just wait until your brothers come, I'll tell them what you've done...'
That evening when her brothers came, the mother told them all.
One took his sister by the hair, another by her hand,
and all night long they beat the girl with a golden rod.
And it was nearing dawn, she was giving up the ghost,
and her mother asked what clothes to lay her out in.
'Do you want your embroidered robes, do you want your silk,
or do you want your green-gold garb I've kept for you in the chest?'
'I don't want my embroidered robes, I do not want my silk,
nor do I want my green-gold garb you've kept for me in the chest.
All I want are these same clothes, the bloodied clothes I wear,
so that the neighbourhood will learn, so the whole land will learn,
how you've unjustly killed me and all for a pair of roses.

Ο Γιάννος και η Μαρουδιώ

Ο Γιάννης με τη Μαρουδιώ σ' ένα σκολειό διαβάζουν.
Γιάννος μαθαίνει γράμματα κι η Μαρουδιώ τραγούδια.
Κείνα τα δυο αγαπιότανε, κανένας δεν το ξέρει.
Και μια Λαμπρή, μια Κυριακή, μια 'πίσημην ημέρα,
ο Γιάννης εξεστόμισε, της μάνας του το λέει.

«Μάνα, την Μάρω ν-αγαπώ, γυναίκα θα την πάρω».
«Τι λες, μωρέ κοψόημερε και φιδοδαγκωμένε;
Η Μάρω είναι ξαδέρφη σου, πρώτη ξαδέρφισσά σου.
Κάλλιο ν' ακούσω σάβανα για να σε σαβανώσω,
παρά ν' ακούσω στέφανα για να σε στεφανώσω».

Η Μάρω αρραβωνιάζεται κι ο Γιάννος αρρωστάει·
η Μάρω στεφανώνεται κι ο Γιάννος ξεψυχάει.
Συμπεθεριό και λείψανο εσυναπαντηθήκαν.
Κανένας δεν αρώτησε από τους συμπεθέρους,
κι η Μάρω ξεδιαντρόπιασε, στέκει και τους ρωτάει.
«Α! τίνος είν' το λείψανο με τη χρυσή την κάσα;»
«Του Γιάννου 'ναι το λείψανο με τη χρυσή την κάσα».

Κι ευθύς σεισμός εγίνηκε και ταραχή μεγάλη.
Βεργολυγάει η λυγερή και πέφτει στο κρεβάτι.
Τα πήραν τα βαριόμοιρα και πάνε να τα θάψουν.
Τα πήγαν και τα θάψανε στης εκκλησιάς την πόρτα.
Μάρω φυτρώνει κάλαμος κι ο Γιάννος κυπαρίσσι,
βεργολυγάει ο κάλαμος, φιλεί το κυπαρίσσι.

Yannis and Maroudio

Young Yannis and young Maroudio were studying together.
And Maroudio was learning song, Yannis was learning letters.
The two of them were deep in love and no one knew of it.
On Easter Day, a fine Sunday, a day to be remembered,
Yannis blurted out his love, he told it to his mother.

'Mother, it's Maroudio I love, it's her I want to marry.'
'What do you mean, you silly fool!—What snake has bitten you?
You know that Maroudio's your kin, you know that she's your cousin.
I'd rather hear of funeral shrouds for me to shroud you with
than to hear of marriage crowns for me to crown you with.'

So Maroudio is betrothed elsewhere, so Yannis starts to sicken,
and Maroudio is married off, and Yannis fades away.
It happened that his in-laws met the funeral procession.
Not one of them thought to ask whose remains they were,
but Maroudio she knew no shame, she stood there and she asked,
'O tell me please whose body lies inside the golden casket?'
'It's Yannis's, they're his remains inside the golden casket.'

And on the spot there was a quake, the entire place was shaken,
the lovely girl bent like a rod and fainted on her bed.
And, ill-fated as they were, they were taken to be buried.
So they were taken, they were buried, right by the church door.
And Maroudio grew as a reed, Yannis as a cypress,
and now the reed bends like a rod, kisses the cypress tree.

Δύο Μαντινάδες

Συ μ' έμαθες πως αγαπούν, πως παίζουν πως γελούνε,
μάθε μου τώρα δυο καρδιές πως ζουν σαν χωριστούνε.

[Κρήτη]

Όταν θα δεις τον ουρανό να βγάλει μαύρο άστρο,
τότε θα σ' αρνηθώ κι εγώ, τριανταφυλλάκι μ' άσπρο.

[Κάρπαθος]

Two Couplets

'Twas you who taught me how to love and live in jubilation,
so teach me then how these two hearts can live in separation.

[Crete]

When you see in the heavens above a black star shows,
it's then I will forswear you, my little, milk-white rose.

[Carpathos]

Rhyming couplets, called *mantinades* in Greek, are still improvised with great skill on the islands of Crete and Carpathos. The first line is usually repeated to give the singer time to find the epigrammatic 'sting in the tail' of the second line. Sequences of *mantinades* can be improvised for hours, with each singer taking their cue from the previous one. These couplets were kindly provided by Bernardo Isola (Crete) and Yannis Philippakis (Carpathos).

LAMENTS AND SONGS OF THE UNDERWORLD

These songs concern death. They are split between songs of the underworld and Charos—the personification of death—and ritual laments.
The former could be recited 'at the table' (*tis tavlas*) or even danced
to at a festival, while the latter could only be performed at a funeral.
Laments were the sole province of women, while songs of the underworld and Charos were usually sung by men.

The word for 'lament' in modern Greek is μοιρολόι (*moiroloi*), literally 'words of fate', referring to the (ancient) concept that the fate of
a person, particularly the moment of their death, has been decided
from birth. Similarly, many of the themes of the laments can be shown
to have their roots in antiquity, as can the funeral rites themselves.
Some of the laments refer directly to particular stages of the funeral.
'The Wooden Horse', for example, would be sung at the preparation of
the coffin. Others, such as the two encomia, in which tribute is paid to
lost beauty, would have been sung at the graveside.

Death, in modern Greek mythology, is unremittingly bleak, wrong
and unjust to the point of perversity. But what is remarkable is how
these songs play out these abstract ideas through dramatic scenes.
Charos is given hugely imaginative guises: from invader ('Charos'
Pavilion'), to pirate ('A Boat Appeared Upon the Shore'), to mounted
horseman ('Charos and the Souls').

Ο Χάρος και αι ψυχαί

Το τι 'ναι μαύρα τα βουνά, και στέκουν βουρκωμένα·
μην' άνεμος τα πολεμά, μηνά βροχή τα δέρνει;
Κι ουδ' άνεμος τα πολεμά, κι ουδέ βροχή τα δέρνει·
μόνε διαβαίνει ο Χάροντας με τους αποθαμένους.
Σέρνει τους νιούς απ' εμπροστά, τους γέροντας κατόπι,
και τα μικρά παιδόπουλα στη σέλ' αραδιασμένα.
Παρακαλούν οι γέροντες, κι οι νέοι γονατίζουν.
«Χάρε μ', γιά κόνεψε σ' χωριό, κόνεψε σ' κρύα βρύση,
να πιουν οι γέροντες νερό, κι οι νέοι να λιθαρίσουν,
και τα μικρά παιδόπουλα να μάσουν τα λουλούδια».
«Κι ουδέ εις χωριό κονεύω 'γώ, κι ουδέ σε κρύα βρύση·
έρχοντ' οι μάνες για νερό, γνωρίζουν τα παιδιά τους,
γνωρίζονται τ' αντρόγυνα, ξεχωρισμόν δεν έχει».

Charos and the Souls

Why are the mountains black and welling up with tears?
Is it the wind that batters them, is it the rain that beats them?
It's not the wind that batters them, it's not the rain that beats them,
it's only Charos passing by, with the dead departed.
He drags the young men out in front, the old men at the rear,
the tender little children all arrayed upon his saddle.
The old men are beseeching him, the young men on their knees,
'Charos, stop at our village—stop at the clear fountain,
and let the elders have a drink, the young men play at quoits,
and let the little children go and gather flowers.'
'I won't stop at your village, nor at the clear fountain,
for mothers come for water there and recognize their children,
and husbands see their wives there too and won't be separated.'

Ένα καράβι στο γιαλό

Ένα καράβι στο γιαλό λεβέντες φορτωμένο,
στην πρύμη κάθοντ' οι άρρωστοι, στην πλώρ' οι λαβωμένοι,
καταμεσής του καραβιού οι θαλασσοπνιγμένοι.
Ντελάλης το διαλάλησε, κι ολούθε το αγρικήσαν:
«Μανάδες, που έχετε παιδιά, γυναίκες, που έχετ' άντρες,
και σεις θλιμμένες αδερφές, πουλιόνται οι αδερφοί σας».
Τρέξαν οι μάνες με φλουριά κι οι αδερφές με γρόσια,
τρέξανε κι οι μαυρόχηρες τα δώρα φορτωμένες.
Μα όσο να φτάσουν στο γιαλό, μίσεψε το καράβι.
Παίρνουν μανάδες τα βουνά κι οι αδερφές τους κάμπους,
κι οι χήρες οι μαυρόχηρες στη μέση του πελάγου.

A Boat Appeared upon the Shore

A boat appeared upon the shore, laden with young men,
the sick were sitting in the stern, the wounded in the prow,
and in the middle of the boat, the ones drowned at sea.
A herald cried, he cried aloud—they heard him everywhere,
'Mothers, who have children, come, women who have husbands,
and all you grieving sisters, come, your brothers are for sale.'
The mothers ran with golden coins, sisters with their silver,
and the black widows ran down too, laden with gifts.
But when they reached the shore, the boat had sailed away.
The mothers make for mountainsides, the sisters for the plains,
and the widows, those black widows, for the middle of the sea.

Η τέντα του Χάρου

Ο Χάρος εροβόλαεν από ψηλή ραχούλα
κι εστέριωσε την τέντα του μέσ' στην απάνω ρούγα.
Άρχοντες τον περικαλούν, φτωχοί τον προσκυνούνε:
«Πάρε, Χάρε, την τέντα σου, πήγαινε σ' άλλη ρούγα,
να φάνε τ' άτια σου ταγή και τ' άλογά σου στάρι,
να φαν και τα ζαγάρια σου αφράτο παξιμάδι».
«Τ' άλογα θέλουν γέροντες, τ' άτια μου παλικάρια,
θέλουν και τα ζαγάρια μου μικρών παιδιών κεφάλια».

Charos' Pavilion

Charos from a lofty peak came roaming down the mountain,
and set up his pavilion in the upper neighbourhood.
The nobles are beseeching him, the poor entreating him,
'Charos, take your pavilion, take it round the corner—
there let your stallions have their food, your horses have their grain,
and let your bloodhounds have their fill of crisp and crunchy rusks.'
'My horses hunger for old men, my stallions for the young,
and my bloodhounds only eat the heads of little children.'

Του Μάη το περιβόλι

Μα του λεβέντη τ' όνομα το πήρε το ποτάμι,
το πήρε και το ξέσυρε στου Μάη το περιβόλι.
Το βλέπει ο Μάης και γελά, η Μάισσα και κλαίει,
το βλέπουν τα Μαγιόπουλα και συχνοκαμαρώνουν.
Κι ο Μάης λέει της Μάισσας, «Τι έχεις εσύ και σκούζεις;»
«Εγώ το νιο που μόφερες το τι έχω να τον κάμω;
Χωρίς σκαμνί δεν κάθεται, χωρίς τάβλα δεν τρώει,
χωρίς μαχαιροπέρουνο δεν κάθεται να φάει,
χωρίς διπλά προσκέφαλα δεν πέφτει να κοιμάται».
«Σύρε, Μαΐτσα μου μην κλαις κι εγώ τον ξεμαθαίνω.
Βάνω τα πιάτα ανάποδα, τα τουβαέλια μαύρα,
βάνω μαχαιροπέρουνα των αντρειωμένων μπράτσα,
του βάνω και ψωμόπουλα μικρών παιδιών κεφάλια».

May's Garden

The young man's name was taken by the river,
which took it and hauled it off into May's own lovely garden.
And May he looks at it and laughs; May's wife starts to weep,
and May's children see it too and they are ever so proud.
And May calls out to his wife, 'Why are you wailing so?'
'This latest youth you've brought me—what can I do with him?
Without a stool he will not sit, won't eat without a table,
without a knife and fork he will not sit for dinner,
without his two soft pillows he will not fall asleep.'
'Come, dear wife, don't cry like that, I'll unlearn him everything.
I put the plates upside down, I make the towels black,
for knives and forks I use the arms of brave men,
for bits of bread, the heads of little children.'

Here the month of May itself is personified and directly replaces Charos, complete with his wife, children and garden. It is no coincidence that 'May's wife' in Greek (Maissa) is the same word as 'witch'. May's family are depicted receiving the dead man into their macabre, topsy-turvy world, with inventive imagery. The motif of a person's 'name' being taken in death is common to other laments.

Το κλειδιά του κάτου κόσμου

Το Χάρο παρεκάλεσα μια χάρη να μου κάμει,
να μου χαρίσει τα κλειδιά να μπω στον κάτου κόσμο.
Και κείνος μ' αποκρίθηκε σα μύριος χαροκόπος:
«Βαριά χάρη μο ζήτησες, καημένη να σου κάμω,
να σου χαρίσω τα κλειδιά να ιδείς τον κάτου κόσμο.
Θα ιδείς τσι νιους και θα σκιαχτείς, τσι νιες και θα λαμπάξεις,
θα ιδείς τσι κουτσοκέφαλους να κόψεις το δικό σου».
Και πήγε και μου τά 'δωκε, να 'θε μη μου τα δώκει.
Κι έβαλα το κεφάλι μου κι είδα τον κάτου κόσμο
κι είδα τσι νιους ξερμάτωτους, τσι νιες χωρίς πλεξίδες,
κι είδα και τα μικρά παιδιά σα μήλα μαραμένα,
κι είδα καλές νοικοκυρές σαν πόρτες γκρεμισμένες.

The Keys to the Underworld

I asked the help of Charos—a favour he would do me—
to let me have the keys to enter the underworld.
And Charos he replied to me, all too cheerfully,
'It's a grave thing you ask of me, poor, wretched girl,
to let you have the keys to see the underworld.
You'll see the young men and take fright, recoil at the maidens;
you'll see them all without their heads, and you'll cut off your own.'
So Charos gave those keys to me, but oh that he had not!
I poked my head inside the place—I saw the underworld:
I saw the young men weaponless, the girls without their braids;
I saw the darling little children rotting like withered apples,
I saw the good housewives like doors torn off their hinges.

Throughout this example, the singer employs puns on the name Charos and the words *chari* ('favour') and *chara* ('joy').

Το κιβούρι της λυγερής

Μαστόροι, που θα φκιάσετε τση λυγερής κιβούρι,
φκιάσ' το πλατύ για τ' αργαλειό, μακρύ για την τυλίχτρα
και στη δεξιά της τη μεριά φκιάστε της παρεθύρι,
να μπαίνει ο αγέρας του Μαγιού κι η πάχνη του χειμώνα,
να μπαιζοβγαίνουν τα πουλιά, να φέρνουν τα μαντάτα·
τι κάνουν νιοι, τι κάνουν νιες, τι κάνουν οι λεβέντες,
τι κάνουν τα μικρά παιδιά, που λείπουν αφ' τσι μάνες,
να με ρωτήσεις να σου πω τι κάνει ο κάτου κόσμος,
που οι άσπροι μαύροι γένουνται κι οι ροδινοί χλομιάζουν,
κι εκείν' οι μορφοσούσουμοι αλλαξομουσουδιάζουν.

The Lovely Girl's Coffin

Craftsmen who will make the coffin of the lovely girl,
make it broad to fit her loom, long to fit her distaff,
and on her right-hand side fashion her a window,
to let the breeze of May come in, the frost of winter enter,
to let the birds come and go, bringing messages:
how the girls are faring there, how the boys are doing,
how the darling little children fare without their mothers;
and if you ask I'll tell you about the underworld,
where the white is turned to black, where the rosy-cheeked pale,
and where the lovely-faced lose their lovely looks.

Πολλά καλά κάνει ο Θεός...

Πολλά καλά κάνει ο Θεός, κι ένα καλό δεν κάνει·
γιοφύρι μες στη θάλασσα και δεμοσιά στον Άδη.
Κι αν δεν εκίναγα να ρθώ, ας μού 'κοβαν τα πόδια,
κι αν δε σε καλογνώριζα, ας μού 'βγαναν τα μάτια,
κι αν δε σ' εσφιχταγκάλιαζα, ας μού 'κοβαν τα χέρια,
κι αν δε σ' εγλυκοφίληγα, ας μού 'κοβαν τ' αχείλι.

Many Are the Good Deeds of the Lord

Many are the good deeds of the Lord, but there's one he doesn't do:
he builds no bridge across the sea, no highway down to Hades.
And if I wouldn't set out on it, let my legs be severed,
and if I wouldn't know your face, let my eyes be gouged,
and if I wouldn't hold you close, let my arms be severed,
and if I wouldn't kiss you sweetly, let my lips be severed.

Δεν είναι κρίμα...

Δεν είναι κρίμα κι άδικο, παραλογιά μεγάλη,
να στέκουν τα παλιόδεντρα και τα σαρακιασμένα,
να πέφτουνε τα νιόδεντρα με τ' άνθη φορτωμένα;

Is It Not Unjust...

Is it not unjust, a crime, a perversion of all reason,
that the old and withered trees stand upright among us
while it's the young trees that fall down, the ones laden with blossom?

Εννιά μοιρολογίστρες

Εγώ ειπα νιος να μη χαθεί και νια να μην πεθάνει
και πάλε οι νιοι για χάνονται και πάλε οι νιες πεθαίνουν.
Εσέ σού πρέπουν, μάτια μου, εννιά μοιρολογίστρες,
οι τρεις από τα Γιάννενα κι οι τρεις από την Άρτα
κι οι τρεις από τον τόπο σου, να ξέρουν τ' όνομά σου.

Nine Lamenters

I said the boy should not be gone, the girl she shouldn't die,
and yet the boys they still are lost, the girls they go on dying.
But you, dear eyes, deserve nine women to lament you,
three of them from Yannena, three of them from Arta
and three of them from your own home, three who know your name.

Το ξυλάλογο

Τώρα είναι το πολύ κακό και το μεγάλο ντέρτι,
που ηφέραν το ξυλάλογο για να το καβαλίκεις
ξεστόλιστο, ξεσέλωτο και ξεκαλιγωμένο.
Γιά πέστε το τού κοπελιού για να το ετοιμάσει,
να βάλει τη χρυσή χασιά, την ασημένια σέλα
και τ' ασημένια πέταλα για να το καλιγώσει.

The Wooden Horse

Now the great evil has arrived, now is the great sorrow,
the wooden horse for you to mount
unadorned, unshod, unsaddled.
So tell the stable boy to prepare, tell him to make it ready,
with the tassels of its golden rug, with its silver saddle,
and tell the boy to shoe it too, with its silver shoes.

The 'wooden horse' here refers to the coffin.

Το μοιρολόγι του Αθανάσιου Διάκου

Μες στ' άμπα του καλοκαιριού και στ' άβγα του χειμώνα,
τήρα καιρό που διάλεξε να πάρει να μισέψει,
τώρα π' ανθίζουν τα κλαριά και λουλουδίζουν κάμποι
κι ανοίγουν τα γαρούφαλα τα μοσκομυρισμένα,
που βάνουν νιοι στα φέσια τους και νιες στες τραχηλιές τους
και τα μικρούτσικα παιδιά να τα κρατούν στα χέρια.

Lament for Athanasios Diakos

At the coming in of summer and the going out of winter,
look at the season that he chose to make his last departure,
now that the branches are in bloom, now that the fields are flowering,
carnations are all opening up and smelling sweet of musk,
boys decorate their fezzes, girls adorn their waistcoats,
and all the darling little children clasp flowers in their hands.

This lament has traditionally been associated with the death of Athanasios Diakos (1788–1821), a hero of the Greek War of Independence, who was put to death by the Ottomans following the Battle of Alamana, April 1821 (see p. 53). The theme of contrasting the renewal of spring with the one-way road of human life and death is common to many laments (including the following one) and belongs to a tradition that far predates the war hero.

Ποντιακό μοιρολόγι

Έρθεν ο Μάρτς κι η άνοιξη κι Απρίλτς κι ο καλοκαίρης
έρται η γη με την χλοήν, τα δέντρα με τα φύλλα,
κι αμάν το ψιλοχόρταρον σκίζ' την ηγήν κι εβγαίνει
τα παλικάρα τα καλά σκίζ'ν την ηγήν κι εμπαίν'νε.

Παρχάρ' και ας έεις το μάραντό σ' κι ας έεις τα μανουσάκια σ'
κι ας έεις τα κρύα τα νερά σ' και τ' έμορφα τ' ομάλα σ'.

Lament from the Pontus

March has come and with it spring, April and with it summer,
the earth is coming into green, the trees coming into leaf,
and as the grass pokes through the earth, pierces it and comes out,
the fine young men poke through the earth, pierce it and go in.
Mountain pasture, keep your narcissus, your never-withering flower,
keep your cooling springs, and your lovely plains.

The Greek of this example is in the dialect of the Pontus—the mountainous
region of north-east Turkey on the Black Sea coast, which was inhabited largely
by Greeks until 1922.

Μανιάτικο μοιρολόγι –Του Γιώργη Σερεμέτη

Παπάδες και πνευματικοί,
τα πετραχήλια βγάλτε τα,
τα θυμιατά πετάχτε τα,
τι εγώ θα κάμω μια γραφή,
ναν τηνε στείλω στην αρχή,
να ρθεί παπόρι στην αυλή,
Ο Γιώργης να μπαρκαριστεί,
ναν τονε στείλω στις Φραγκιές,
οπού είναι οι τέχνες οι πολλές,
ναν τονε μπαλσαμώσουσι,
κι απέ ναν τονε φέρουσι,
ναν τονε βάλου στον οντά,
να είμαι κι εγώ νοικοκυρά...

Τύφλες και μαύρα φάσκελα!

Lament from the Mani—for Yorgis Seremetis

Priests, confessors, clergymen,
take off your vestments,
put down your incense,
for I am going to write a note
and send it to some potentate
and in the yard will come a boat
and Yorgis will get on and float
all the way to the Frankish West,
where they do those crafts the best,
and there his body they'll embalm
then bring him back into my arms.
I'll set him in the finest hall
and I'll be Lady of it all...

O what nonsense, what foolish drawl!

The laments from the Mani region of the southern Peloponnese have their own
tradition. The metre is different from the standard folk song metre, being made
up of eight-syllable iambic lines with strong rhyme between them. The content
is largely improvised and relates to the specific person—rather than making
use of the established themes of the other laments. This example is short—
Maniat laments can run for hundreds of lines.

Εγκώμιο για μια κοπέλα

Χριστέ, τι νια που χάθηκε κι όμορφα δεν την κλαίτε,
όπου της πρέπει τέτοιας νιας δικό της μοιρολόι,
που 'χε το Μάη στσι πλάτες της, την άνοιξη στα στήθια,
που 'χε του ήλιου τσ' ομορφιές, του φεγγαριού τσ' ασπράδες,
του μήλου του βενέτικου τσι ροδοκοκκινάδες,
που 'χε τα μάτια δυο ελιές, τα φρύδια δυο γαϊτάνια,
τα δόντια πυκνοφύτευτα σαν τα μαργαριτάρια,
που 'χε το μέλι στην καρδιά, την ζάχαρη στα χείλη,
είχε και μες στο στόμα της το μόσκο φυτεμένο,
που 'χε της χήνας το λαιμό, της πέρδικας τα στήθια.
Στη γης μη την πιθώσετε χώμα να τηνε φάει.
Φκιάσε της κάσα ολόχρυση και κάσα κρουσταλλένια,
να πά' να την πιθώσετε στου Μάη το περιβόλι,
να πέφτουν τ' άνθια απάνου της, τα μήλα στην ποδιά της,
τα κόκκινα γαρούφαλα τριγύρω στα μαλλιά της.

Encomium for a Girl

Christ, what a girl that's gone, and you don't weep beautifully,
but a girl the like of this one deserves her own lament—
for she had May upon her back and spring upon her breasts,
she had the beauties of the sun, the moon's own whitenesses
and like a fine Venetian apple the same rose-rednesses;
for she had eyes like olives, silk tresses were her eyebrows,
a row of densely planted teeth like pearls packed together;
for she had honey in her heart and sugar on her lips,
her breath was fragrant as musk,
her neck slim as a goose's neck, her breasts like partridge breasts.
So don't lay her in earth, don't let the soil consume her.
But make a casket all of gold, make a crystal casket,
and lay her down on the grass, in May's own lovely garden,
so that the blossom falls over her, apples in her apron,
and let the red carnations lie strewn around her hair.

Εγκώμιο για ένα αγόρι

Αχ νεέ μου ηλιογέννητε κι ηλιοσκαμαγκισμένε,
το δέντρο δέντρο πάηνες το πυκνοφυτεμένο,
μη σε λερώσει ο κορνιαχτός, μη σε μαράν' το κάμα
γιατί 'σουν νεός και νεούτσικος, γιατί 'σουν παλικάρι,
και δεν σου πρέπει για τη γης και για το μαύρο χώμα,
ότ' είσαι νεός και νεούτσικος, είσ' αρραβωνιασμένος.
Αχ νεέ μου χαμπηλόζωστε, ψηλά ανασκουμπωμένε,
μουστάκι μου καραμπογιά και φρύδια μου γραμμένα,
πού να σειστείς να λυγιστείς και πού να καμαρώσεις
και πού να βρεις μακρύκαμπο να παίξει τ' άλογό σου;
«Μαύρη μου, όσα κι αν μου πεις, όλα χαμένα τά 'χεις
εδώ νέοι δε χαίρονται, νέοι δεν καμαρώνουν,
εδώ το λεν στο χαλασμό οπού χαλνούν ο κόσμος,
χαλνούν των μάνων τα παιδιά, των γυναικών οι άντρες».

Encomium for a Boy

O boy, born of the sun, your sun-bleached hair wool-tousled,
from tree to tree you went for shade, under the tree's thick shade—
O let the dust not speckle you, the heat not wither you,
for you were young, so very young, you were a fine young man,
the earth's no fitting place for you, the black earth doesn't suit you,
for you were young, so very young, engaged to be married.
O boy with your low-slung belt, standing tall and proud,
with your pitch-black moustache, the fine-drawn lines of eyebrows,
where can you sway and pace, where can you dance so proudly,
and where can you find a long meadow for your horse to play in?
'Black-clad woman, what do you mean, you've lost your wits!
Here the boys take no joy, here the boys aren't proud,
here they call it ruin, here where the world is ruined,
the mother's children here are ruined, and men who once had wives.'

Ατός μου τό 'δα τ' όνειρο...

Ατός μου τό 'δα τ' όνειρο πού 'θελα να πεθάνω,
κόκκινα είδα κ' εφόρηγα, πράσινα και γεράνια·
το πράσινο ήτανε κακό, το κόκκινο χαμπέρι,
κείνο το καταγέρανο Χάρος που θα με πάρει.
Εψές προψές επέρασα στου Χάρου τα λημέρια·
ακούω νταούλια να βροντούν και μπαταριές να πέφτουν.
Κάνε σε γάμους πέφτουνε, κάνε σε πανηγύρια;
Μάιδε σε γάμους πέφτουνε, μάιδε σε πανηγύρια.
Μια χήρα κάνει μια χαρά παντρεύει τον υγιό της,
σφάζει γουβάλια τριανταδυό, γουβάλια τριανταπέντε.

I Dreamed I Was to Die

I dreamed of it myself—I dreamed I was to die,
I saw red—I was wearing red—and green and deep night-blue.
The green meant evil, the red meant news,
and that deep blue was Charos who would take me.
Yesterday, the day before, I passed by Charos' lair,
I heard drums pounding there and I heard volleys firing:
are they firing at some wedding, or at some festival?
They're not firing at some wedding, nor some festival,
but there's a widow having a feast, she's marrying off her son,
butchering thirty-two buffaloes, butchering thirty-five.

INDEX OF GREEK TITLES

NOTE ON SOURCES

The first published collection of Greek folk songs was by a French scholar, Claude Charles Fauriel (1772–1844), who collected songs from expatriate Greeks of Trieste and Greek intellectuals in Paris. His *Chants Populaires de la Grèce moderne* (1824) is still considered one of the most authentic folk song collections, and I have drawn on it extensively in this anthology, particularly for the songs of brigands. Subsequent collections also came from the hands of foreign Philhellenes—notably those of the German Theodor Kind (1835) and Italian Niccolò Tommaseo (1842), who collected songs from his native Venice.

Interest from Greek scholars began slightly later, with Spyridon Zambellios (1813–81), who was born on Lefkas into the enlightened environment of the Ionian Islands. Zambelios was the first to locate the missing link between ancient and modern Greece in the times of the Byzantine Empire, specifically in the folk songs (and in the texts of the church). This book contains two songs from his collection of folk songs, published in 1852. It was also in that year that Nikolaos G. Politis (1852–1921) was born. Politis is considered the founder of Greek folklore studies, and was the first to give a Greek term to the discipline: *laografia*, from *laos* ('people') and *grafo* ('write'). The most widely read and loved of his works is his *Selections of the Songs of the Greek People*, published in 1914. Some of the songs in this book are drawn from that collection.

The majority of the songs, however, are from anthologies that have taken their material principally from the archive of the Hellenic Folklore Research Centre. These include the series entitled *Το δημοτικό τραγούδι* ('The Folk Song') published by Estia Publications; *Ελληνικά δημοτικά τραγούδια: Τα Μοιρολόγια* ('Greek Folk Songs: Laments'), Nefeli Publications, 2000; *Ελληνικά δημοτικά τραγούδια (εκλογή)* ('Greek Folk Songs: A Selection'), Academy of Athens, 1962.

MODERN
GREEK
CLASSICS

Rebetika: Songs from
the Old Greek Underworld
BILINGUAL EDITION

Translated by Katharine Butterworth & Sara Schneider

The songs in this book are a sampling of the urban folk songs of Greece during the first half of the twentieth century. Often compared to American blues, rebetika songs are the creative expression of people living a marginal and often underworld existence on the fringes of established society.

C.P. CAVAFY
Selected Poems
BILINGUAL EDITION

Translated by David Connolly

Cavafy is by far the most translated and well-known Greek poet internationally. Whether his subject matter is historical, philosophical or sensual, Cavafy's unique poetic voice is always recognizable by its ironical, suave, witty and world-weary tones.

ODYSSEUS ELYTIS
1979 NOBEL PRIZE
In the Name of Luminosity and Transparency

With an Introduction by Dimitris Daskalopoulos

The poetry of Odysseus Elytis owes as much to the ancients and Byzantium as to the surrealists of the 1930s, bringing romantic modernism and structural experimentation to Greece. Collected here are the two speeches Elytis gave on his acceptance of the 1979 Nobel Prize for Literature.

NIKOS ENGONOPOULOS
Cafés and Comets After Midnight
and Other Poems
BILINGUAL EDITION

Translated by David Connolly

Derided and maligned for his innovative and, at the time, often incomprehensible modernist experiments, Engonopoulos is today regarded as one of the most original artists of his generation and as a unique figure in Greek letters. In both his painting and poetry, he created a peculiarly Greek surrealism, a blending of the Dionysian and Apollonian.

M. KARAGATSIS
The Great Chimera
Translated by Patricia Barbeito

A psychological portrait of a young French woman, Marina, who marries a sailor and moves to the island of Syros, where she lives with her mother-in-law and becomes acquainted with the Greek way of life. Her fate grows entwined with that of the boats and when economic downturn arrives, it brings passion, life and death in its wake.

STELIOS KOULOGLOU
Never Go to the Post Office Alone
Translated by Joshua Barley

A foreign correspondent in Moscow queues at the city's central post office one morning in 1989, waiting to send a fax to his newspaper in New York. With the Soviet Union collapsing and the Berlin Wall about to fall, this moment of history would change the world, and his life, forever.

ANDREAS LASKARATOS
Reflections   BILINGUAL EDITION
Translated by Simon Darragh

Andreas Laskaratos was a writer and poet, a social thinker and, in many ways, a controversialist. His *Reflections* sets out, in a series of calm, clear and pithy aphorisms, his uncompromising and finely reasoned beliefs on morality, justice, personal conduct, power, tradition, religion and government.

MARGARITA LIBERAKI
The Other Alexander
Translated by Willis Barnstone and Elli Tzalopoulou Barnstone

A tyrannical father leads a double life; he has two families and gives the same first names to both sets of children. In an atmosphere of increasing unease and mistrust, the half-siblings meet, love, hate, and betray one another. Hailed by Albert Camus as "true poetry," Liberaki's sharp, riveting prose consolidates her place in European literature.

ALEXANDROS PAPADIAMANDIS
Fey Folk
Translated by David Connolly

Alexandros Papadiamandis holds a special place in the history of Modern Greek letters, but also in the heart of the ordinary reader. *Fey Folk* follows the humble lives of quaint, simple-hearted folk living in accordance with centuries-old traditions, described here with both reverence and humour.

ALEXANDROS RANGAVIS
The Notary
Translated by Simon Darragh

A mystery set on the island of Cephalonia, this classic work of Rangavis is an iconic tale of suspense and intrigue, love and murder. *The Notary* is Modern Greek literature's contribution to the tradition of early crime fiction, alongside E.T.A. Hoffman, Edgar Allan Poe and Wilkie Collins.

EMMANUEL ROÏDES
Pope Joan
Translated by David Connolly

This satirical novel and masterpiece of modern Greek literature retells the legend of a female pope as a disguised criticism of the Orthodox Church of the nineteenth century. It was a bestseller across Europe at its time and the controversy it provoked led to the swift excommunication of its author.

ANTONIS SAMARAKIS
The Flaw
Translated by Simon Darragh

A man is seized from his afternoon drink at the Cafe Sport by two agents of the Regime by car toward Special Branch Headquarters, and the interrogation that undoubtedly awaits him there. Part thriller and part political satire, *The Flaw* has been translated into more than thirty languages.

GEORGE SEFERIS
Novel and Other Poems
Translated by Roderick Beaton

1963 NOBEL PRIZE
BILINGUAL EDITION

Often compared during his lifetime to T.S. Eliot, George Seferis is noted for his spare, laconic, dense and allusive verse in the Modernist idiom of the first half of the twentieth century. Seferis better than any other writer expresses the dilemma experienced by his countrymen then and now: how to be at once Greek and modern.

MAKIS TSITAS
God is My Witness
Translated by Joshua Barley

A hilariously funny and achingly sad portrait of Greek society during the crisis years, as told by a lovable anti-hero. Fifty-year-old Chrysovalantis, who has recently lost his job and struggles with declining health, sets out to tell the story of his life, roaming the streets of Athens on Christmas Eve.

ILIAS VENEZIS
Serenity
Translated by Joshua Barley

The novel follows the journey of a group of Greek refugees from Asia Minor who settle in a village near Athens. It details the hatred of war, the love of nature that surrounds them, the hostility of their new neighbours and eventually their adaptation to a new life.

GEORGIOS VIZYENOS
Thracian Tales
Translated by Peter Mackridge

These short stories bring to life Vizyenos' native Thrace, a corner of Europe where Greece, Turkey and Bulgaria meet. Through masterful psychological portayals, each story keeps the reader in suspense to the very end: Where did Yorgis' grandfather travel on his only journey? What was Yorgis' mother's sin? Who was responsible for his brother's murder?